P9-CRL-956

Facts and Fallacies of
International Business

HF1455
F3

Facts and Fallacies of International Business

■■■■■■■■■■■■■■■■■■■■■■■■■■■■■■■

JOHN FAYERWEATHER

MANAGING EDITOR

The International Executive

75673

OCT 1962

HOLT, RINEHART AND WINSTON   •   NEW YORK

To My Mother-in-Law
LILLIAN L. SELINA
A Loyal and Kindly Friend

COPYRIGHT © 1962 BY JOHN FAYERWEATHER

ALL RIGHTS RESERVED

LIBRARY OF CONGRESS CATALOG CARD NUMBER 62-12204

22760-0112

PRINTED IN THE UNITED STATES OF AMERICA

382
F296

■■■■■■■■■■■

Preface

The tremendous expansion of American overseas business in the postwar era has evoked a very mixed public response. At home, our international operations have been alternately praised for their economic contributions and harassed with charges of "exporting jobs" and "evading Treasury agents in tax-haven countries." Abroad, American capital has been enticed and applauded for its role in industrial development at one moment, and in the next breath criticized and threatened by nationalists charging it with economic imperialism.

That the public should have a superficial, and often confused, picture of such matters is neither new nor surprising. It has been characteristic of international trade issues throughout our history. The average man gives little time or thought to the issues because they usually concern affairs which are remote from his life and involve fairly complex economic and business arrangements. They are matters of intense personal concern to a few people, such as manufacturers threatened by imports or lawyers protecting a favorable tax arrangement; and these people devote tremendous effort to arguing the merits of their case, often with heavy appeals to emotion at the expense of objective statement of facts. Thus the public hears little except the impassioned declarations of the special pleaders on either side.

As in many public issues, the truth lies somewhere between the extreme views which flow so glibly from the political rostrum and the daily press. There is much that is good and useful in our international business and there are clearly points at which its actions create problems for society. My purpose in this book is to scrutinize carefully each of the aspects of international business which has caught the public eye, summarizing the charges which have been leveled, stating the facts that bear on them, and drawing what I feel are the justifiable conclusions.

The chapters are written with an eye to maximum clarity and readability for the general reader. Toward this end statistical and technical details have been kept to a minimum. For those who wish to pursue any aspect at depth, supplemental information is provided at the end of the book. The Appendix contains the most important sets of statistics pertinent to our international business. The references list books and articles covering detailed studies of subjects discussed in each chapter.

Although each chapter may be read separately, they follow a general pattern. The first four deal with the major phases of the flow of international business: exports, imports, and overseas operations. These lay a foundation for the fifth chapter on the balance of payments, which draws together all the threads of our transactions with the rest of the world. The sixth chapter, analyzing the dollar problem, is a sequel to the fifth. Chapter 7, on East-West trade, is an independent issue. The next three chapters deal with key aspects of management of our extractive and manufacturing operations in foreign countries.

I have drawn on help, information, and wisdom of many people in putting this book together. The specific contributions are acknowledged in the text. Here I want to express my appreciation to a handful of friends who played a major part in bringing the book into being.

First and foremost, I owe a great debt to my wife, who found time amidst the responsibilities of a mother and editor to help in a multitude of ways. Her encouragement set the project in motion and her suggestions throughout have been an immense help.

Second, Florence Keller and Isabel Lynn provided that underlying administrative support without which a modern author is lost — accuracy and promptness in turning out a steady flow of fresh manuscript.

Third, I owe much to Emile Benoit and Richard Robinson, who read the whole manuscript and made a number of suggestions. Although I could not agree with their opinions in all respects, their comments resulted in many improvements in the book.

Having noted the welcome aid of these associates, I must immediately emphasize that the responsibility for the content of the book is entirely my own.

New York, N.Y.   *J.F.*
March, 1962

■■■■■■■■■■■

Contents

	Preface	v
1	Are We Exporting Jobs?	1
2	The Battle for Exports	12
3	The Tariff Question	31
4	Havens from the Harsh Tax Winds	50
5	Our Unbalance of Payments	65
6	On the Brink of Bankrputcy	91
7	Trading with the Enemy	101
8	The Lingering Curse of Exploitation	120
9	Fears of Economic Imperialism	137
10	Carrots and Umbrellas	150
11	A Look Ahead	165
	References	168
	Appendix	174
	Index	181

■■■■■■■■■■ *1*

Are We

Exporting

Jobs?

"Entirely too much of the present outflow of [investment] funds is going into manufacturing facilities. This has the effect of setting up competition for our exports, particularly to Europe and the United Kingdom. Total sales of American plants in Europe in 1959 amounted to about $8 billion. Certainly part of this $8 billion worth of merchandise could have been replaced by exports of American-manufactured items. I think it is unnecessary to point out that these extra exports could have balanced our payments and provided additional jobs at home."—Senator Albert Gore (D. Tennessee), Congressional speech, January 9, 1961.

This is the "overseas manufacturing exports American jobs" thesis. It has gained wide acceptance, because of the combined impact of high domestic unemployment and the United States balance of payments deficit. As no early solution to either of these problems is in prospect, it is likely to be a prominent feature in public debates for some time to come.

On the surface, Senator Gore's position is persuasive. One of the few aspects of international business upon which there is full agreement is the steady shift from export to foreign manufacture. In country after country products that used to be imported from the United States are now made by local factories. A few years ago, Caterpillar Tractor Company had but one foreign factory, in Glasgow, Scotland. Now it has plants in Australia, Brazil, and France, each making bulldozers, graders and other pieces of equipment that used to be exported from the United States. Right after

1

World War II Philco shipped its radios and refrigerators from American factories to customers all over the world. Today Philco subsidiaries in Mexico, Brazil, and a number of other countries are supplying their markets with locally made appliances. This type of transition to foreign manufacture has taken place in the operations of practically every American company engaged in international business.

In each shift, some work required to make products in the United States for export ceases to exist and is replaced by work in overseas factories. A bulldozer exported to Brazil is put together by workers in Peoria, Illinois, while one manufactured locally takes Brazilian labor. When Philco stopped exporting radios to Mexico, the work that had been done by assembly-line operators in Philadelphia was taken over by new workers in the plant in Mexico City.

The transition to foreign manufacture and the displacement of American labor when a product is shifted from export to overseas production are readily apparent. Putting them together, it is easy to leap to the Senator's conclusion that if the process of foreign

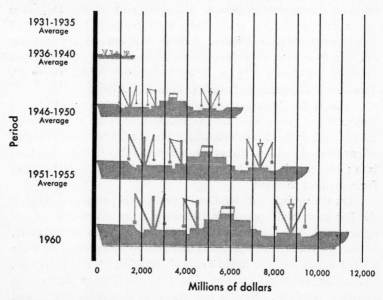

FIG. 1. United States exports of finished manufactured goods (in millions of dollars).

Source: See Appendix, Table 1.

investment were checked, American jobs would be saved. But the story is by no means as simple as that.

The Trend of Our Trade

A few facts outlining the evolution of the pattern of our overseas business in manufactured products will provide a good starting point for unraveling this story. As Figure 1 shows, our exports of finished manufactures have almost doubled since the end of World War II, rising from a 1946–1950 average of $6,576 million per year to $11,435 million in 1960.

The output of American overseas factories was not reported in government statistics until 1957, so we must judge the trend prior to that by the investment figures charted in Figure 2. In the postwar

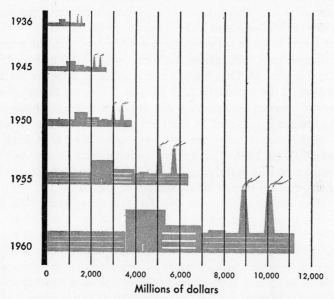

FIG. 2. United States direct investment in overseas manufacturing (in millions of dollars).
Source: See Appendix, Table 3.

era manufacturing investments have almost quadrupled from $2,854 million in 1946 to $11,152 million in 1960. In 1957 our manufacturing units overseas had a production volume of $18.3 billion.[1*] By

*References are listed at end of book, following Chapter 11.

1960, their output had risen 30 percent to $24 billion. In over-all terms it is clear that, while overseas manufacture has grown more rapidly and now overshadows exports in magnitude, there has not been an absolute loss of exports in this period.

Looking at specific industries we find a more confused picture. Some show a notable increase in exports. Chemical specialities, for example, rose from an average of $155 million between 1946 and 1950 to $663 million in 1960 as industrial expansion abroad created a demand for a wide range of the products of advanced American chemical research. Industrial machinery exports increased from an average of $1,178 million in the 1946–1950 period to $2,529 million in 1960. During 1960, foreign orders were accounting for about one third of the total business of the American machine tool industry. Industrialization in the underdeveloped countries and the European boom stimulated sales of the great assortment of machines of which the United States is the dominant producer.

Exports in other industries have not fared so well. Shipments of passenger cars, for example, declined from 153,000 units in 1950 to 145,000 units in 1960, though the increase in prices raised the value from $179 million to $235 million. Data on output of all American overseas auto plants is not available, but a good measure of the change is indicated by the increase in General Motors cars and trucks manufactured abroad from about 200,000 in 1951 to about 800,000 in 1960. The rapidly growing market for automobiles overseas, especially in Europe, is being supplied for the most part by products made in foreign plants and not by export.

These statistics spell out in concrete form the generally observed evolution in our trade patterns. As sales have expanded, overseas manufacture has become common for many products which a few years ago were major export items. At the same time export sales of specialized products in such areas as machinery, electronics, and chemicals have increased. Industrialization abroad has expanded the demand for these products but not yet to the point where manufacture is considered.

Could the Jobs Be Saved?

This evolution of our trading patterns explains why total exports have grown despite the shift from exports to overseas manufacture. The steady increase of export sales in the specialized products has covered over the decline in products like automobiles. Taken by themselves, the statistics for this declining group provide a harsh and solid base for the exporting-jobs argument. Looking at the automobile situation, for example, one might readily agree with Senator Gore's conclusion that if GM had not expanded its plants abroad so rapidly, a large number of men would have been employed in Detroit making cars for export to the burgeoning foreign market.

Digging still deeper into the facts, however, we find that the switch to overseas manufacture has generally been a forced one and that in many cases it has actually preserved exports which might otherwise have been lost.

By and large, American manufacturers would rather make products in the United States and export them abroad. This arrangement minimizes the various economic and political risks which are substantial in many of the less-developed countries and exist to some degree even in Europe and Canada. It simplifies operating control and utilizes capacity most effectively.

Each of Caterpillar Tractor Company's plants abroad is exposed to some risk. In Brazil, political upheaval is a constant possibility, and the country's financial condition is precarious. Australia, Britain, and France are politically more stable but each has had financial problems which create some risk for Caterpillar. And from a management control point of view it would be much simpler to have all the operations in Peoria. Much duplication in production equipment and personnel could be eliminated and facilities could be utilized more efficiently. For example, during the 1960–1961 recession, sales in the United States fell off but they were booming abroad. With operations centralized in one plant, production volume could have been balanced better as sales in some areas of the world rose and in others fell. All in all, life would be much simpler and safer for the Caterpillar management if it did not have plants scattered around the world.

Thus the first instinct of most managements is to stick with exporting, and the decision to manufacture abroad is usually made with reluctance to meet the economic necessities of the current world situation. A large portion of the foreign factories have been set up because of import restrictions which threatened to cut off export markets completely. In an extensive study of investment decisions by E. R. Barlow and Ira T. Wender, 48 percent of the companies said they were "forced to invest to maintain markets."[2]

In the typical case a country anxious to develop its local industry or to save foreign exchange imposes or threatens to impose import restrictions. The American company has the simple choice of starting manufacture or losing the market.

In earlier years, American businessmen often looked upon import restrictions as temporary checks and they were slow to move into manufacturing. H. J. Heinz II relates such an experience of his company in Australia.[3] The company had built up a good market for its soups. In 1931, import restrictions were imposed suddenly, cutting off the market. Heinz did not decide to go into manufacturing in Australia until 1935. By then it found that the reputation it had built up for its brand name by years of promotion had largely been lost. Ten years of patient rebuilding were needed to establish the company's market position again.

Made wiser by experiences like this, most United States companies now accept the fact that import controls are likely to be a permanent barrier and they had best undertake manufacture to protect their businesses. To avoid having to start up production on a crash basis, managements try to get their manufacturing plans going somewhat before controls actually hit them. This is usually quite practical because most foreign governments give ample early warnings. For many months and often years before imports are stopped, government officials will indicate their intentions by suggestions, threats, and other signals designed to push the companies into local manufacture. Oftentimes the future course of government policy is clearly set out in industrial development plans which state the products for which it intends to promote local production. The handwriting is on the wall. To avoid a hasty decision under pressure, to get a jump on other manufacturers, or to make a good impression on the government, the American company starts manufacturing.

Stories in this pattern can be related by practically every American company operating abroad. The experience of the XYZ Drug Company in India is typical. The company's sales grew quite rapidly after World War II but they were still so small that local production would have cost more than importing products made in the United States. Thus the market was served by exports from the United States. The Indians had import restrictions, however, which kept the XYZ Company from importing as much as it could sell. Furthermore, the economic development plans of the government gave a high priority to manufacturing pharmaceutical products. The import control officials seemed to be clamping down harder, and other government men made repeated suggestions to the effect that it was high time the drug companies started manufacturing. There were several other United States and British drug companies selling in India and the XYZ management was concerned about what might happen if one of these companies started manufacturing.

Consequently, in 1950, John Thomas, the XYZ international vice-president, decided it would be wise to make the jump into manufacturing. The company developed a plan to make a few of the simpler drugs and took it to the Indian government. The officials were not happy because they thought still more products should be made but they did agree to the plan. They assured that import controls and tariffs would be set up in such a way that XYZ could set prices high enough to make a profit even though its costs were higher than in the United States. Mr. Thomas had some trouble convincing the XYZ board of directors that the investment should be made. The board members felt that the financial risks in India and the possibilities of the country going over to the Communists made the investment a poor idea. However, Mr. Thomas was able to persuade them to go along with the plan. The plant was set up in 1953 and subsequently it has taken on the manufacture of additional drugs.

In the XYZ case and in many other similar manufacturing decisions, the loss of American exports could have been postponed. Probably a year or two might have elapsed before XYZ would have been actually forced to make its move. But the ultimate loss is inevitable and for the company the effort to shift its operations in an orderly way before the government acts is sound.

Besides these import restriction situations, there are a large number of manufacturing investment decisions which are responses to basic cost-profit economics. As sales abroad have expanded, large-scale production with cost savings is possible. The economies of production, combined with lower transportation costs and lower wages, have made supplying certain markets from overseas factories more profitable than export from the United States. The typewriter business is a notable case in point. In 1960 both Smith-Corona and Remington Rand switched their production of portable typewriters from plants in the United States to European factories where costs were lower.

Such profit-oriented decisions might seem to be exactly what Senator Gore is inveighing against. The implication is that American capital is deliberately cutting down American exports and thus jobs solely for selfish profit motives. In the current rough world competition, however, it is more a decision for survival than for greater profit. A company which sticks to export when the economics favor overseas manufacture runs a good chance of losing its market completely to competitors. It may be to another American company or it may be to a German or perhaps a Japanese company. But there are so many aggressively investing international companies today that it is safe to assume that any cost advantage from overseas manufacture will be quickly seized by someone. Thus, the company which does not capitalize on cost advantages from overseas manufacture is not in the long run helping to save American exports.

The decisions of Smith-Corona and Remington Rand seem, if anything, to have been dangerously slow. European firms like Olivetti were making deep inroads into the market for portable typewriters both in the United States and in foreign markets. The American companies had already lost a great deal of ground and were not operating profitably. Smith-Corona had a large loss in 1960. Underwood, after years of deficits, had been bought by Olivetti in 1959. Thus the shift to European production was long overdue and essential to meet the low-cost competition of our world competitors.

Virtually all overseas manufacturing investment decisions will fit into one of these broad categories, with the hand of management forced either by immediate or prospective restrictions or by the inexorable power of cost-profit economics. Rarely, therefore, can one assume, as Senator Gore has, that a decision has been made to start manufacturing while exporting was still quite practical. In many cases the exports might have continued for a while, perhaps even for a few years, but such a decision would be counter to sound business and ultimately undesirable for the U.S. world commercial position.

The Case of the Auto Industry

A further look at the automobile industry illustrates these points very clearly. With the exception of a few factories in Europe, GM, Ford, and Chrysler supplied foreign markets before World War II with exports from the United States using assembly plants in larger countries. After the war, studies made by these companies indicated that this was still the most economical system and they sought to continue it. But a variety of circumstances has forced them to take a different course in country after country.

Shortly after the war, Australia decided it wanted a locally manufactured car and would stop all imports. General Motors accepted this challenge despite the small market which would make local production more costly than importing. It developed the Holden car, which has been a tremendous success, generating large profits which ultimately benefit the United States balance of payments. The other American companies had to abandon the market. They have now belatedly re-entered it and are struggling to gain a piece of the market dominated by Holden. It is fairly safe to assume that had GM not developed the Holden, one of the British companies would have taken up the government proposition and the United States would have lost not only the export market but also the chance to earn profits on the investment. This, in fact, is what did happen in India.

In 1954, the Indian government gave the auto companies the choice of starting to manufacture or getting out. The annual sales by all companies in India at that time were about 30,000 cars, far below the volume of any one plant in the United States and the prospect of much increase seemed quite distant. Ford and GM decided that local manufacture at that level was so economically undesirable that it would be unsound for India as well as for themselves. So they refused to undertake manufacture. It is quite possible that they thought the government would back down, as a key government adviser and others were in agreement with their analysis. The government stood its ground, however, and the two major American companies departed, leaving the market largely to British and German companies.

In the main Latin-American countries, the American companies have been under varying degrees of government pressure to increase the number of locally manufactured components used in cars. At first, the companies resisted this pressure strongly, arguing as in India that it was economically unsound. However, they have steadily come around to conformance with the governments' wishes, prompted especially by the aggressive invasion of these markets by the German and Italian companies. Fiat, Volkswagen, and others have moved quickly and effectively into local manufacture, sometimes in partnership with the local governments. Despite belated efforts to make up for lost time, the American companies have lost a substantial share of the markets, especially in Brazil and Mexico, to these competitors.

The evolution of the automobile industry in Europe is all too familiar to the American public. The little Volkswagens, the Citroens, the Fiats, and others, which populate our highways are ample evidence of the economic competitiveness of local manufacture in Europe. The market for cars in most European countries has now expanded to the point where a considerable degree of mass production is possible. This, combined with wages a half to a third of those in Detroit, gives European manufacture a strong cost-profit edge over products made here. Thus the American companies have had no choice but virtually to abandon export to Europe, expanding their factories to produce there and even to import into the United States.

With minor variations, this story could be retold for most of our export industries: farm equipment, radios, drugs, and so on down the line. It is not a "good" story in that export jobs have clearly been lost. But it is equally clear that insistence by the companies on sticking to exports would not have saved the jobs. On the brighter side, we can see in this evolution opportunities for sustaining some American employment through export of parts and machinery, which is the other major aspect of the subject overlooked by Senator Gore.

Keeping Our Share

When manufacturers of other countries take over a part of our export market, our loss is usually complete because they draw all the imports they need from their home bases. For example, when the Fiat automobile plant in Mexico needs tools or dies or parts, it buys them from Italy. And, similarly, where we have held markets by establishing factories we retain at least a portion of our export volume. Sometimes the portion is large. The American automobile plants in Mexico, for example, still import a large percentage of their parts besides some specialized machinery. In other cases, such as soap manufacture, the percentage is small, but even there the needs for machinery are significant.

The total benefit to our exports from this source is impressive. According to the 1957 government census, American overseas operations purchased 10 percent of their material requirements from the United States. Thus, approximately $2 billion of our exports were sold to our overseas factories in the form of parts, basic chemicals, and so on. The census figures do not include purchases of plant equipment, but, according to a *Business Week* study, 40 percent of the $1.7 billion of new capital sent overseas for direct investments in 1960 was in the form of American machinery and other exports.[4] Setting these figures beside our total exports of around $20 billion per year, we can see that the fact that American companies have invested abroad rather than allowing markets to be lost to foreign competitors has been a notable factor in sustaining our exports.

Making the Best of a Changing World

The substitution of overseas manufacture for exports is not desirable either for individual companies or for the country as a whole. But it is an inevitable adjustment to the growing and changing world economy. Far from being an avoidable form of "exporting jobs," it is the only way we can hold our share of world markets against foreign competition and it permits us to keep a significant volume of exports in the form of machinery and materials that otherwise would be completely lost.

■■■■■■■■■■ *2*

The Battle
for Exports

Have we, like Frankenstein, created a monster through our foreign economic policies?

This question has haunted many Americans in recent years. Ominous signs have appeared suggesting that in trying to be helpful and constructive we have created a giant with two powerful arms which are slowly destroying our export trade. On the one hand, there are fears that the surge of industrial development abroad which we have encouraged and aided may displace our exports from overseas markets. On the other, there are worries lest our products be frozen out of the groupings of countries into common markets to which we have given our blessing.

Our Sagging Export Status

This concern arises from tangible evidence of weakness in our exports. As we noted in Chapter 1, American exports have risen since World War II. But the rise has been relatively modest compared with the growth of world trade as a whole, especially during the past few years. As Figure 3 shows, we have been steadily losing ground in competition with other nations as an exporter of manufactured goods. Although we accounted for almost 26 percent of total manufactured exports in 1953, our portion had shrunk to 21.3 percent in 1959. In the same period other countries made notable gains: West Germany from 13.3 to 19.1 percent, Japan from 3.8 to 6.7 percent, and so on.

12

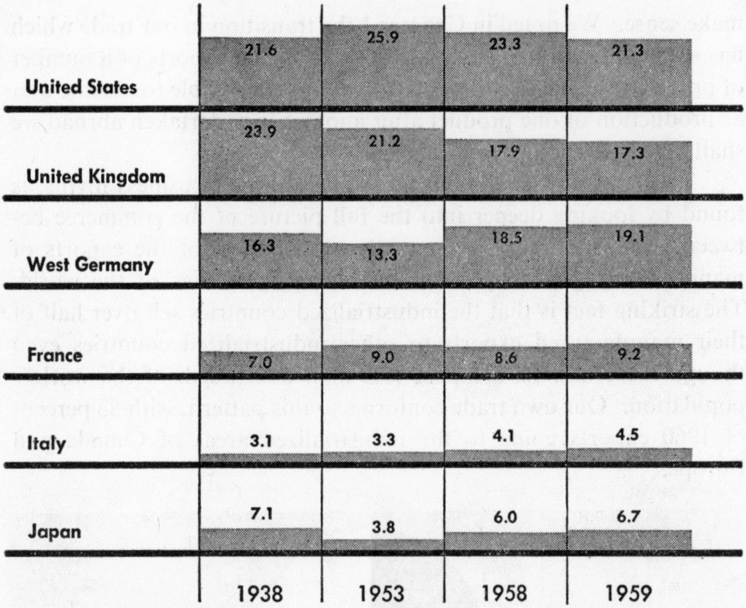

United States	21.6	25.9	23.3	21.3
United Kingdom	23.9	21.2	17.9	17.3
West Germany	16.3	13.3	18.5	19.1
France	7.0	9.0	8.6	9.2
Italy	3.1	3.3	4.1	4.5
Japan	7.1	3.8	6.0	6.7
	1938	1953	1958	1959

FIG. 3. Percentage of total world exports of manufactured goods.
Source: United Kingdom Board of Trade Journal.

Some people say we need not be too concerned because these changes simply mark the return to prewar trading patterns. Comparison with the 1938 data supports their view. Our current percentage is now roughly the same as it was in 1938. But the late thirties, combining a major depression in the United States and German and Japanese war preparations, was scarcely a normal period. Furthermore, the determination of what is "normal" is not very relevant in any case. The important point is that we have lost ground at a time when we badly need export income to strengthen our balance of payments. So we need to look critically at the problem to see why it has developed and what can be done about it.

Is Overseas Industrialization a Threat?

International business is bedeviled with a number of myths which cause considerable trouble because superficially they appear valid. Not the least of these is the idea that as industrialization abroad grows, our exports must suffer. At first glance this seems to make sense. We noted in Chapter 1 the transition in our trade which has resulted in overseas manufactures replacing exports of a number of products, such as automobiles. Is it not reasonable to assume that as production of one product after another is undertaken abroad we shall slowly lose our export markets?

The fallacy in this, as in most international business myths, is found by looking deeper into the full picture of the commerce between nations. Figure 4 shows the distribution of the exports of manufactured goods by the industrialized countries of the world. The striking fact is that the industrialized countries sell over half of their manufactured exports to other industrialized countries even though these nations compose less than one fourth of the world's population. Our own trade conforms to this pattern, with 53 percent of 1960 exports going to the industrialized areas of Canada and Europe.

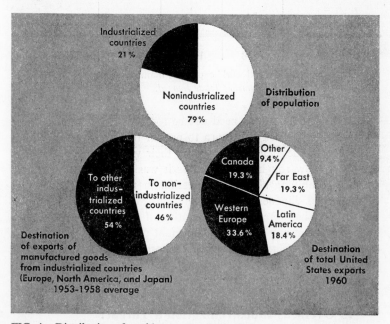

FIG. 4.   Distribution of world exports and population.
Sources: International Trade, 1955 and *1959,* GATT, and Appendix, Table 2.

The same point is made with equal emphasis by comparing the magnitude of our exports to different countries. Within each geographical area, our exports are greater on a per capita basis to the countries with the greater per capita income, which is a good measure of their degree of economic development. For example, we see in Figure 5 that United States exports to our northern neighbor in 1960 worked out to $208 per individual Canadian while to Mexico we shipped only $24 worth of goods per individual Mexican. The reason lies in the increasing volume and variety of needs which accompany economic growth and in the specialization of the industries of each nation. The whole Canadian population enjoys a standard of living close to that of our own people. They do, of course, make a large portion of the products they consume, but the proliferation of demands is always running ahead of Canadian manufacturing capabilities. So they are a receptive market for a host of American products from industrial machinery to 8mm movie cameras.

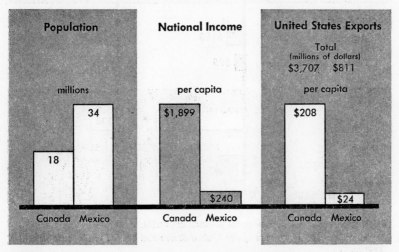

FIG. 5.   United States exports to Canada and Mexico, 1960.
Sources: Statistical Abstract of the United States and *United Nations Statistical Yearbook.*

Most Mexicans, on the other hand, are still at a very low standard of living. Although the country has little productive capacity by comparison with Canada and has to import a large portion of its requirements, especially of manufactured goods, its capacity to purchase is relatively much smaller. Accordingly our exports to Mexico on a per capita basis are only one eighth of the flow to Canada. Similar comparisons appear among the different nations of Europe, South America, and the Far East, shown in Figure 6.

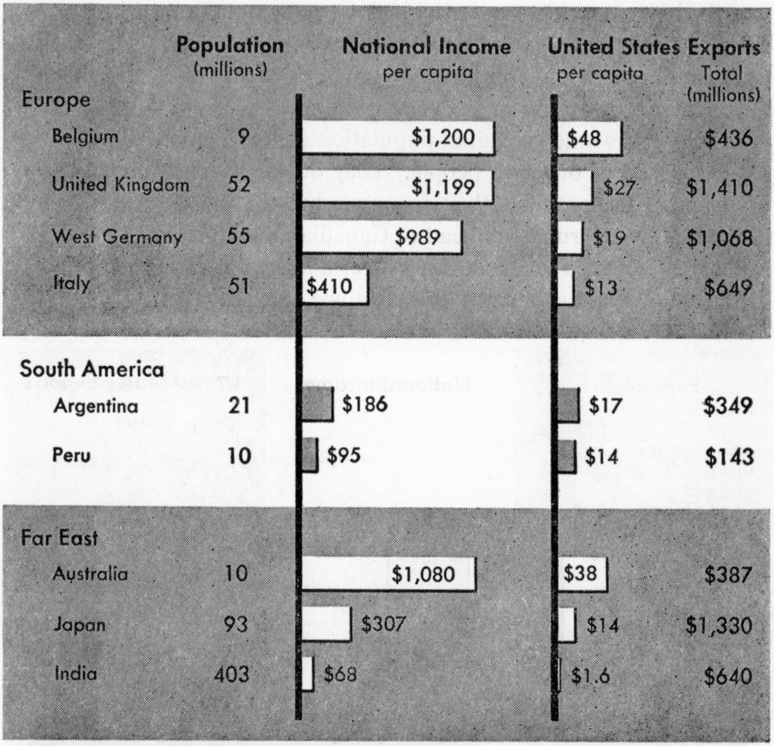

	Population (millions)	National Income per capita	United States Exports per capita	Total (millions)
Europe				
Belgium	9	$1,200	$48	$436
United Kingdom	52	$1,199	$27	$1,410
West Germany	55	$989	$19	$1,068
Italy	51	$410	$13	$649
South America				
Argentina	21	$186	$17	$349
Peru	10	$95	$14	$143
Far East				
Australia	10	$1,080	$38	$387
Japan	93	$307	$14	$1,330
India	403	$68	$1.6	$640

FIG. 6.   United States exports to selected countries, 1960.
Sources: Statistical Abstract of the United States and United Nations Statistical Yearbook.

The shift from export to overseas manufacture of automobiles, radios, and other specific products discussed in Chapter 1 is thus just one phase of the total evolution of trading patterns. More important for our export status is the general rise of foreign living standards, which carries with it an increase in export volume of a broad range of products. The surge of industrialization is not only not a cause for worry; it is a source of bright promise for the future. From the statistics in Figure 6, it is staggering to consider how much our exports may be increased if, for example, the 400 million Indians could be lifted to something close to the standards of the Australians.

Today the average Indian with an income of $68 a year may buy a razor, some medicine, and a few other items beyond the necessities of food and clothing. He supports a small American export volume in pharmaceuticals, machinery used to make locally manufactured products, and some other items. But the volume is insignificant compared with what it could be at a higher standard of living. Then, as with Australia, we would be shipping more consumer products, ranging from drugs to cameras and still greater amounts of industrial goods: electric computers, chemical specialities, machine tools, and a host of others. Today we export a mere $1.60 of goods per capita to India, but with the tremendous population there that still means $640 million a year. If the per capita income in India could be doubled to a still modest $150 per year, with a comparable rise in imports, it would increase our national exports by $640 million, a very substantial gain.[1]

From these facts we may reasonably conclude that in fostering economic development abroad we have in fact helped our total export volume to increase. We must therefore look at other factors to find a cause for the decline in our relative export status.

The Price Question

The most widely accepted explanation for our weakened position is that "we are pricing ourselves out of world markets." A study by Emile Benoit comparing the trend of prices and costs in the United States with that of other countries gives strong credence to this thesis.[2] Figure 7 gives some typical figures of changes from 1953 to 1959. Other indices or years would show differences in degree but not in the basic pattern.

The composite index of the prices of manufactured goods which we export rose about 16 percent from 1953 to 1959, while similar indices rose 5 percent for Germany and 10 percent for the United Kingdom, and dropped 5 percent for France. The differences show up clearly in the trends of prices of industrial goods made in the United States and of those imported into this country from European countries. Domestic steel bars cost 29 percent more in 1959 than in 1953 while imported bars went up only 8 percent in price. Prices of cement made in the United States rose 24 percent in the same period

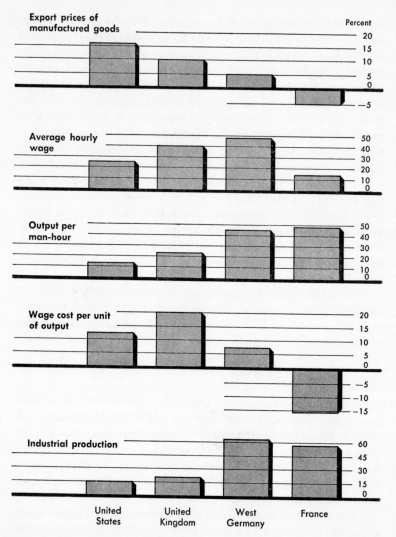

FIG. 7.   Changes in price, cost, and production indices from 1953 to 1959.
Source: Emile Benoit, *Europe at Sixes and Sevens.*

but the cost of European imported cement actually dropped 15 percent. Thus for product after product it is quite evident that our export competitors have been gaining ground on us in prices.

Behind these price trends are changes in costs. Hourly wages have actually gone up faster in most European countries than have those in the United States. Wages in Germany, for example, rose almost 50 percent in the 1953–1959 period while ours increased half as much. But the big difference is the rapid increase in productivity in Europe. The average worker in the United States turned out only 13 percent more production every hour in 1959 than in 1953. But the German workers increased their individual output by 44 percent in that period; the French workers, by 48 percent. In industry after industry European factories have been able to show impressive gains in productivity relative to the United States.

Steel plants in Europe have been able to increase production volume sharply with little increase in labor forces. At the same time, American steel mills have been making much slower progress in raising the output of each blast furnace crew, each open-hearth furnace, and so on. The actual productivity of most European industries is still below that of American plants. For example, the Inland Steel Company plant in East Chicago, employing about 18,000 workers, produces 4.7 million tons of steel per year, while the Dortmund-Horder plant in Germany has only slightly fewer workers — about 17,000 — yet makes only 2.5 million tons per year.[3] But the changes in productivity indicate that the margin is narrowing.

Because of this improvement in productivity most of the European countries show an advantage in the change in wage cost per unit despite the increase in hourly wages. The average German worker producing, let us say, steel bars, received almost 50 percent more wages per hour in 1959 than in 1953. But because he had increased his output of bars each hour by almost as much, the bars were not costing the manufacturer much more than in 1953. In the United States, on the other hand, the hourly output of steel workers has gone up very little; hence the wage increases have resulted in substantial rises in costs. As a result of similar conditions throughout American industry, the index of wage costs per unit of output rose 12 percent in the United States while it increased only 7 percent in Germany and declined in France. It is significant to note that the United Kingdom, which is also having balance of payments troubles these days, showed a greater increase in unit wage costs than did the United States.

The explanation for the differences in productivity appears to lie in the comparisons at the bottom of Figure 7. While industrial production rose 15 percent in the United States, the European countries were experiencing a great boom that carried Germany ahead by 62 percent, France by 57 percent, and so on. Currently many industries in the United States are operating at 10 to 15 percent below desired capacity, while most European plants are running at full blast and are unable to meet demand. In the United States we have a 6 to 7 percent unemployment compared with a critical labor shortage in most of Europe.

Thanks to this rapid build-up of production, the Germans and other Europeans have been able to use their plants, equipment, and labor to maximum effect, whereas our idle capacity is a burden on the costs of our production. The heavy fixed costs of highly mechanized modern plants put great premium on keeping volume at a peak. To appreciate the importance of these costs one need only observe the impact of business cycles on the profits of American companies. For example, the 1960 sales of General Electric were only 4 percent below 1959 but the profit fell 29 percent. In the previous year, sales had risen 6 percent but profit jumped by 16 percent.

This sort of arithmetic has been working to the advantage of the Europeans operating for a sustained period at full capacity. They have been able to turn out production at minimum cost while our output has carried a substantial cost load of idle capacity. The steel industry is an excellent case in point. American steel mills have been running far below their potential volume for several years. In 1961, their output ranged from 50 to 70 percent of potential capacity. But, because of the nature of steel operations, their labor costs have been considerably more than 50 to 70 percent of what they would be at 100 percent of capacity. A steel mill that uses 500 men to run at 50 percent of capacity can push production up to 100 percent of capacity with only a small increase in work force. We can see the nature of the problem in the employment data of the industry in the latest two consecutive nonstrike years. From 1957 to 1958 steel-ingot production fell from 107 million to 81 million tons, a 24 percent decline. Yet the man-hours of worker employment dropped only from 986 million to 956 million, a mere 3 percent. The European mills operating close to capacity have therefore been using their manpower much more efficiently.

The European boom might never have started without the $11 billion of American aid under the Marshall Plan. In addition, the Europeans have benefited from the lower costs of more modern facilities in some industries which were almost completely reconstructed after the war, often with Marshall Plan money. But to say that these dollars have boomeranged in the form of lower-cost European export competition is to take a very narrow view of the situation. For one thing, we owe a substantial part of our current exports to the boom. For example, exports of machine tools, chiefly to Europe, have been accounting for 30 percent of our industry's sales.

But more important is the evidence that our trouble lies in weaknesses at home, in the sluggishness of our own economy; hence our efforts at correction had best be in that direction. It may be that the Europeans' cost advantage has already run its course because of the strong wage demands from scarce labor and because future increases in production must come from more costly expansions of factories. Regardless of that situation, however, our best hope lies in revitalizing our own economy so that unemployment drops, demand increases, and our plants come closer to capacity production. It is, of course, impossible in this book to discuss the various means for accomplishing that end, but it is reassuring to know that this need is recognized by most of our national leaders and that the debate among our political parties on the subject is primarily over differences in methods rather than over objectives.

Giving Exports a Push

In addition to the basic cost-price question, there are two other factors which have undoubtedly contributed to the relatively better export performance of our competitors: effort and government help.

Stories making unfavorable comparisons between the export sales efforts of Americans and their competitors are legion. A typical one cites the experience of a Mexican who wrote to an American company and to a German one about buying some new machine tools. A week later two Spanish-speaking salesmen from the German firm arrived offering advice and good financing terms. After another week passed a catalogue in English arrived from the American company, along with a letter giving the name of a distributor in Mexico City whom the Mexican could see if he was interested.

The story may be fiction but the picture it conveys is not. Although there are many exceptions, American companies generally do not apply as much effort to export sales as our competitors for the simple reason that exports are not so important to us. Whereas exports account for 24 percent of gross national product for Germany and 13 percent for Japan, they compose only 4 percent of our GNP. Working down to individual cases, we find the typical American manufacturer exporting perhaps 10 percent of his output while his German and Japanese competitors export 25 to 50 percent of their production.

The impact of these figures is felt all through the organization. The president of a German company making lathes and drills gives personal attention to export sales; tools are redesigned to fit special needs in other countries; production plans are adjusted to facilitate exports; the best personnel are assigned to sell overseas and are given strong support. In a comparable American company the president gives casual attention to export work (as compared with overseas investments, which have a higher priority of interest); products are designed for the domestic market with minor export modifications when they are absolutely necessary (for example, 220-volt transformers are added to electric appliances in countries having that type of electric power system); export orders are fitted into production schedules as best they may after domestic needs are met; and the export manager is a subordinate cog in the managerial hierarchy, constantly suffering from lack of support from above.

The shortcomings of such a situation are illustrated by the Paulman Company, whose three divisions made a number of specialized textile products.[4] The export manager, Mr. Wilson, was under the supervision of Mr. Rayburn, the general manager of Division 1, which had the largest export volume, but his section also exported the products of Divisions 2 and 3. Mr. Rayburn was agreeable in his relations with Mr. Wilson but paid little attention to his work.

Mr. Horn, the manager of Division 3, was quite uncooperative. Export orders for Division 3 products were consistently set aside until all domestic customers were served; hence the foreign shipments were often long delayed. In addition, Mr. Horn insisted that the export department quote prices that provided an extra margin of profit to make up for the nuisance he felt the foreign sales involved.

Mr. Wilson tried to improve the situation by obtaining a favorable directive from the president of the company, Mr. Higby. Mr. Higby agreed in principle that there should be no discrimination against export orders, but Mr. Horn, who was higher on the management ladder than Mr. Wilson, outmaneuvered him. In a private conversation Mr. Horn told Mr. Higby that he also agreed with the principle of not discriminating against export orders and suggested certain revisions in the directive which, he said, would make it more workable. In fact, the changes were just enough to put Mr. Wilson right back where he started and he was out in the cold. Mr. Higby had so many bigger concerns that he did not want to discuss it further with Mr. Wilson. Mr. Rayburn did not care enough about the problem to go to bat for Mr. Wilson. So the export side of the business kept on being treated like a stepchild.

Many American companies have not even had enough interest in exports to try to develop any overseas business. Selling abroad means adding new people who know how to handle the operations. It also involves dealing in foreign exchange, doing business under new laws, and coping with a variety of other complications which are discouraging, especially to a small company. There are a large number of concerns which, like the Paulman Company, are in exporting but not wholeheartedly. Only a few of our companies can really be classed as first-rate export businesses.

In the decade following World War II our export business prospered despite these management weaknesses. The demand for American products and the lack of strong competition from other countries were such that American products sold readily abroad. But the surge of competition from European and Japanese companies has put the spotlight on our deficiencies and stimulated considerable interest in improving our performance.

The United States government, the United States Chamber of Commerce, and a number of other organizations have undertaken a variety of efforts in this direction. The government launched an "Export Expansion" program in 1960. Considerable publicity has been devoted to the need to export more and to the opportunities which exist for American business. Seminars and other meetings have been organized to stimulate greater interest in exports, to persuade top executives to give exporting a higher priority, and to assist companies to start up export departments. It is hard to change the attitude of American industry appreciably, however, for even a significant increase in exports will not raise them to anything like the importance they command in the operations of our European and Japanese competitors.

The Export Expansion program leads us into the area of

government help to export operations. There have been notable differences in the extent to which American firms and their competitors receive assistance, particularly in financing and field support. Most foreign governments back up the financing of their exporters in substantial terms. The German government, for example, working through a semiofficial organization called Hermes, will insure 70 to 80 percent of the risks in any export sale. Thus a German exporter selling a machine to a Brazilian can assume greater risks or allow the Brazilian longer to pay for the machine. If he were selling on his own, he would have to worry more about the political hazards and the instability of the Brazilian currency. He might have to require the Brazilian to pay 50 percent of the price of the machine immediately and the balance within a year. But with Hermes assuming most of the risk he can afford to take a 10 percent down payment and let the Brazilian pay the rest over three years. Naturally his chances of selling the machine to the Brazilian are better when he gives the more liberal terms.

The United States government for many years abstained from this sort of help except for long-term financing of major capital goods, such as electric power plants through the Export-Import Bank. In 1960 the policy was changed as one means to foster exports, and the Ex-Im Bank started underwriting shorter-term transactions for a wide range of products. There was still a difference, however, particularly in the fact that the Ex-Im Bank covered only the *political* and not the *commercial* risks for short-term financing. The exporter could be protected from loss due to political trouble — for example, debts which could not be collected because of the Cuban revolution. But the bank could not insure against failure of the customer to pay. A German firm could obtain both types of protection.

Late in 1961 our government took a long step to eliminate this disadvantage for our exporters. The Ex-Im Bank joined with a group of fifty-seven private insurance companies in a joint insurance system for short- and medium-term export credits. The companies composing the Foreign Credit Insurance Association (FCIA) do the actual insuring, with the Ex-Im Bank backing them up. For a short-term credit (up to 180 days) the exporter must himself assume 5 to 10 percent of the political risk (inability to convert foreign currency into dollars, cancellation of import licenses, political difficulties, and the like) and 15 percent of the commercial risks (insolvency or default of the buyer). The Ex-Im Bank underwrites the remaining

90 to 95 percent of the political risk and the Bank and the FCIA share equally in 85 percent of the commercial risk. Medium-term credits (180 days to 5 years) are handled in essentially the same manner except that the foreign buyer must make a down payment of 10 percent, which is not required for the short-term insurance. This new system is designed to permit American exporters to offer financing terms on essentially the same basis as their foreign competitors offer.

The question of field support has followed much the same pattern. The governments of most countries assume a more active role in the development of export trade than does ours. They have men in their embassies and consulates who devote their careers to trade development. These specialists are constantly looking for opportunities and they participate directly in arranging trade negotiations for their countrymen. A German machine manufacturer interested in business in Brazil, for example, knows he has an active agent in the German consulate in São Paulo, the industrial center of the country. The German representative will be constantly on the lookout for possible machinery sales and he will see to it that the leads are communicated directly to the manufacturer and to other German companies when he sees promising situations. When the German exporter goes to São Paulo, the government man will give him detailed advice on sales prospects, take him around to meet potential customers, counsel him as needed during subsequent negotiations, and, finally, help out if problems develop after the German exporter goes home.

The United States government also assists our exporters, but the contribution made by our field representatives has been substantially less. Partly this has been a matter of ability. The typical commercial man in our embassies is a State Department officer trained for political work. The commercial assignment has usually been for a three- to four-year period, not long enough to develop real competence or interest in business. Partly it is a matter of deliberate policy. Our philosophy tends toward minimizing the direct help of government to the businessman. Thus our commercial officers have been told that they should not enter directly into the development of specific trading opportunities and their budgets do not permit sufficient time, in any case, for such work. The belief has generally prevailed that the businessman can and should do a better job of developing trade on his own and that intervention by the government involves risks of partiality to one or another exporter at the expense of others.

As a result, American companies have received a good deal less help than have their counterparts from Germany and other countries. Our commercial officers do look out for opportunities, but they have had little time for such work; hence for the most part they know only of needs which are reported directly to them by local companies who take the initiative in coming to our embassies with inquiries. These opportunities are reported back to Washington and published in *Foreign Commerce Weekly*, a magazine put out by the Department of Commerce. The alert exporter will check it regularly, but this reporting system is slower and less complete than an advice sent direct to the manufacturer. When the export manager of an American machinery company goes abroad, the commercial officer in our embassy has usually talked to him about conditions in the country. He has given him a list of companies who are potential customers and may have introduced the businessman to a few of them. But he has been hard-pressed for time to do even this much. Furthermore, most of the commercial officers have been men with little business know-how; hence the American exporters have not felt that these officers really could be of much more help even if they did have the time.

Since 1960 there has been a shift in these practices in the direction of greater aid. Although the commercial officers will still be State Department employees, they are being trained by the Commerce Department and will make careers of commercial work. There will be more of them and their activities will involve somewhat greater direct help to the exporter. Still they will probably not go so far as the representatives of many competing nations, who will do practically everything up to the point of writing a sales order for one of their exporters.

Underlying the government support situation are basic differences in national and government philosophy. In general, Americans have an aversion to "government in business," our business community prefers to manage its own affairs, and the government is reluctant to do anything which might be labeled "helping special interests." In application, these principles become muddled by competitive pressures and national needs. As a result we end up with policies which are a compromise — enough to take some of the edge off the criticism that Germans and others have too much advantage over our exporters, and yet not enough really to equalize the competitive situation.

The Common Market: Boon or Bogy?

One of the most extraordinary developments of our times is the "common market." Efforts toward liberalization of trade among nations have been gaining support since the mid-thirties. But the common market concept goes far beyond liberalization: it involves a deliberate blending of national economies and even political union. This is such a sharp break with the centuries-old drive toward independent nationalism that it must stand as a revolutionary turning point in history.

The most advanced of the common markets is the European Economic Community established by the Treaty of Rome, signed in March, 1957. The members compose the so-called "Inner Six": France, West Germany, Italy, Belgium, the Netherlands, and Luxembourg. Most of the other important European nations are grouped into the European Free Trade Association (EFTA) under the Stockholm Convention signed in November, 1959. Its members, often called the "Outer Seven," are the United Kingdom, Sweden, Norway, Denmark, Switzerland, Austria, and Portugal. The future of EFTA is uncertain because the United Kingdom applied for admission to EEC in 1961. Other EFTA countries are expected to follow Britain's lead. If they are admitted, EFTA may break up, with most of its members joining EEC.

Other common markets are far less advanced. In 1960 a Central American group was set up including Guatemala, Nicaragua, Honduras, and El Salvador, with Costa Rica and Panama likely to join. It had started functioning by 1961. The Latin American Free Trade Association (LAFTA) was formed in 1960 by Argentina, Brazil, Chile, Mexico, Paraguay, Peru, and Uruguay, with initial tariff reductions scheduled for 1962. It has not made much tangible progress however, and, since 90 percent of the members' trade is with nonmember nations, it may not be too significant in any case. Other groupings in the embryonic stage are the Casablanca bloc (Egypt, Morocco, Ghana, Guinea, Mali, and Algeria), the Monrovia group (Nigeria, Liberia, and several former French colonies in West Africa), and the Association of Southeast Asian States (Philippines, Thailand, and Malaya).

Each of these groupings has its own characteristics but as far as

American exports are concerned, they all pose essentially the same question: what effect will tariff changes have on our competitive status? We can, therefore, concentrate on one group only and, as the European Common Market (EEC) is the most fully developed example, it makes the best subject of discussion.

Although the Rome Treaty covers a number of phases of economic unification, including labor and capital movements, antitrust laws, and agricultural policies, its primary immediate objective is the creation of a customs union. By 1973, the members are (1) to eliminate all tariffs and other restrictions on trade with each other; and (2) to establish a single tariff system for trade outside the EEC, with most rates equal to the average of the existing rates of the members. The treaty set up a schedule, which has subsequently been accelerated, for accomplishing these objectives by stages. Whether the full transition will be completed before 1973 and whether the United Kingdom and other nations will be included soon are at this writing uncertain. But the prospects for ultimate achievement of a full customs union are promising.

How will this affect our exports? The most obvious effect is that within each EEC nation our exports must compete against exports from other EEC countries at a tariff disadvantage. For example, prior to EEC, both American and German machinery paid the same duty of about 15 percent to enter France. By 1961 the Germans were paying 30 percent less tariff and eventually they will pay none. Meantime, as the EEC average is about equal to the French rates, American companies would continue to pay a 15 percent duty and thus have a 15 percent disadvantage against the Germans. Determining the potential loss of exports from this cause is a difficult job involving thorough analysis of the composition of existing trade. Emile Benoit, after a penetrating analysis of the question, has concluded that the United States might lose from 5 to 10 percent of its exports to the EEC countries in this way or $120 to $240 million per year.[5]

Counterbalancing this potential loss is a possible gain which we may have already started to realize. This is the benefit from the acceleration of the economic growth of the EEC countries, which is projected at around 5 percent per year, compared with the 3 percent long-term growth for the United States. The current boom which was mentioned above is in part due to the stimulation to investment from the prospect of broadened markets for EEC countries. German companies foresee bigger sales in France, French companies forecast increases in German sales, and so on. The combined effect is a significant increment to the already sharp rise in European production and from this we benefit in larger sales of machine tools, chemicals, and other products.

The full potential which may be realized from the accelerated economic growth involves so many variables that it cannot be predicted with accuracy. Professor Benoit did not attempt any estimate in his study, but he does conclude from an analysis of the products in our trade that there are good prospects for increases in over a third of the exports and these could well offset the 5 to 10 percent loss estimated above.[6] The European countries are deficient in most foods and raw materials, and as their rates of consumption increase so will their needs for imports. Our present shipments in these items are already large. We exported $479 million of raw cotton and $540 million of grain to Western Europe in 1960. Any substantial increase in such large blocks of our exports would greatly improve our over-all export picture. And, as we have noted, the European demand for specialized manufactured exports is already good and can be expected to rise.

On the whole, therefore, the development of common markets need not be looked upon as a threat to our exports. But that does not mean we should not be concerned about their tariff policies, which result in discrimination against us as compared with members. Every effort should be made to bring the external tariffs of EEC and other common markets down. The prospects of progress in this direction are encouraging. After extended negotiations with the United States government, the EEC countries agreed in early 1962 to a 20 percent reduction in their external tariffs on a wide range of industrial products and made concessions on agricultural imports which affect about half our exports of foodstuffs to Europe. Further reductions might have been achieved had the United States nego-tiators been in a position to offer greater, across-the-board tariff cuts, a question discussed in the next chapter. With this favorable attitude among European countries, it will be fruitful for the United States to adopt new tariff legislation which will give our government suitable bargaining power and to pursue every opportunity for further reductions.

Tinkering with the Mechanism

Ten years ago American exports were booming, limited only by the amount of dollars other countries could earn. Today we are fighting to hold our own in competition with European and Japanese companies and there is widespread worry lest we be losing ground in the struggle. Yet between these two periods the statistical differences are actually quite modest. Our total trade has grown substantially and our percentage of the total world trade in manufactures has slipped somewhat less than 20 percent.

In assessing our situation we need to keep the whole process of world trade in perspective. The system by which it stays in approximate balance is something of a miracle. In a period which has included the reconstruction of Europe, the emergence there of a revitalized economy and the organization of the common market, the resurgence of Japan, and strenuous economic development efforts in the less-developed countries, it is scarcely surprising that there should be times when the trade of some nations gets out of balance.

We should not be complacent when the balance tips against us, but it is reassuring to see how the basic system is able to right itself over the course of time. We may consider, for example, how the Europeans and the Japanese have been able in a few short years to strengthen their own export position so much. It is quite within our power, therefore, to swing the pendulum in the opposite direction; not all the way, for that would simply put our competitors back in their initial hole, but far enough to ease our current strain. What is needed is a little tinkering with the system to help the natural adjustment process: some measures to stimulate our home economy to increase productivity and lower our costs and prices, a greater export effort by our manufacturers, a moderate increase in the help our government gives our exporters in financing and personal aid in the field, and continuing pressure on evolving common markets to reduce their external tariffs.

■■■■■■■■■■ *3*

The
Tariff
Question

"We've had to lay off eighty workers since sports shirts began coming in from Hong Kong. We just can't meet the prices of people who can hire labor for 12 cents an hour. That's not fair competition. We need protection."

If you are a reasonably decent human being, this plea of a typical protection-seeking American industrialist strikes a sympathetic chord. You're sorry for the Chinese, but after all why do they have any more right to jobs than the Americans the manufacturer had to lay off? It's nice to have cheaper shirts but it's pretty selfish to put a fellow American out of a job to save a few cents. And, what's more, it might be your job that's in danger next, considering the rate the foreigners are importing new things into the United States. So why not go along with the protection idea, tariffs or quotas or whatever will help?

This intermixture of facts, logic, and sympathy underlies the protectionist sentiment in the United States, which seems to be growing in strength. The last major tariff increases came in the Smoot-Hawley Act of 1930. In 1934, a period of reductions started with the passage of the Trade Agreements Act inspired by Secretary of State Cordell Hull. Under its authority, successive administrations, both Republican and Democratic, have worked our tariffs down to a relatively low level. The protectionist opposition has been continuing and bitter, however, and violent debates in Congress and throughout the nation arise each time our national trade policy comes up for review.

How Much Protection?

Over-all, our tariffs are not large in relation to our volume of trade. In 1959 our imports totaled $15 billion, and the customs service collected $1 million of duties. That works out to about 7 percent of the value of the total imports, compared to 25 percent in 1933. But these over-all figures are not very meaningful because the rates vary greatly among products.

For a large portion of American trade, tariffs are not significant. About 40 percent of our imports bear no duty, notably products like coffee of which there is little or no domestic production. A substantial number carry moderate duties which are an impediment to trade but not a major obstacle, for example automobiles, 8 percent; steel products, 5–10 percent; and aluminum, 5 percent.*

The real protection is found among the products with higher rates, such as 20 to 30 percent for cotton fabrics, 30 percent for coal-tar chemicals, and 50 percent for watches.* The degree of actual protection afforded depends upon the costs in each industry. There are some cases in which tariffs effectively exclude imports. For example, miniature balls used in the points of ball-point pens carry duties up to 1400 percent. There were a number of prohibitive tariffs like this a few years ago but most of them have been drastically reduced since World War II. In other instances, the tariff is not high enough so that American manufacturers can compete. Jewel bearings for watches have a 10 percent tariff, but the Swiss can make bearings at prices considerably lower than 10 percent under American costs; hence there is virtually no American production, and all our requirements are filled by imports.

For most of the larger protected industries, the existing rates come reasonably close to equalizing American and foreign costs. In some cases, the tariff permits high-cost American producers to compete with lower-cost imports. In others, American products, through strong brand preference or through some other marketing advantage, survive despite somewhat lower prices on foreign-made goods. As a result, some American manufacture continues along with a considerable flow of imports, as indicated by the figures from an analysis of 1954 data by the Brookings Institution.[1]

---

*These are approximate average rates for categories of imports. The duties for specific products within each category vary according to characteristics and prices.

Commodity	Average duty (percentages)	United States Production Imports (millions of dollars)		Imports as percentage of United States production (percentages)
Zinc	6%	$205	$34	16%
Unmanufactured wool	13	91	60	66
Hatters' fur	16	9	0.5	6
Motorcycles and bicycles	12	88	29	33
China and earthenware	50	115	18	16
Musical instruments	19	36	13	35
Leather gloves and mittens	35	43	2.5	6

It is around the rates for these industries that the main debate swirls. The importance of the products in the economy is sufficient so that supporters of liberal trade policies can argue for broad benefits from lower duties with reduced retail prices. At the same time, the manufacturers, supported by their labor unions, have enough hope and resources to fight to maintain their precarious position.

Although tariffs are our chief form of trade restriction, we must consider as part of this subject quotas and "Buy American" regulations. Quotas provide protection for some of our largest industries. Imports of petroleum are limited to about 10 percent of our requirements under a federal control system. Venezuelan and Middle Eastern oil costs much less than our crude; hence without the quotas foreign oil would take over much of the American market and many domestic producers would be pushed to the wall. The cotton textile industry has gained at least partial relief from the influx of Japanese fabrics through a quota system arranged with the Japanese government.

The "Buy American" regulations apply to purchases by the United States government. Their purpose is to give American companies a preferred position in supplying government needs. The degree of preference has varied since the idea was first adopted by Congress in 1933. Currently, all domestic bidders on federal contracts are allowed a 6 percent advantage over foreign concerns, and those located in the numerous economically distressed (surplus labor) regions of our country receive an additional 6 percent (12 percent total). The most publicized application of the Buy American regulations has been in the sale of turbines and other large pieces of equipment for electric power-generating plants. Big power units are not mass-produced; hence labor composes a high portion of their cost of manufacture. Lower wage levels, combined with high industrial productivity in Europe and Japan, mean that foreign producers can often underbid General Electric, Westinghouse, and other American companies. For example, in 1953 a British firm bid 20 percent under the lowest American offer on $6 million worth of equipment for the Chief Joseph Dam on the Columbia River, and a British bid of $13 million for a steam generator for the Tennessee Valley Authority's Greer's Ferry project in 1954 was $6.3 million below our best bid.[2] But with the margin provided by the Buy American act the domestic firms have been able to win the majority of United States contracts.

Who Is Hurt?

Determining exactly the extent of possible injury from the removal of tariffs and other restrictions is not possible because no one knows how much domestic business would be displaced. If we include such large industries as textiles and petroleum, several million workers are directly or indirectly involved in fields having some sort of protection. Oscar R. Strackbein, long the most vocal representative of protectionist interests, claimed in Congressional testimony that 5 million jobs were directly vulnerable to import competition and that 15 million were indirectly endangered.[3] But it is very unlikely that so many jobs are actually dependent upon protection.

More realistic figures are provided by three research studies. The first, by Walter Salant of the Brookings Institution, determined that for every $1 million increase in imports an average of 103 workers would be displaced among the 72 import competitive industries.[4] The second study, by Mordechai Kreinin of Michigan State University, concluded that the broadly applied 15 percent tariff reductions made in 1956 resulted in a $200 million increase in imports.[5] If the Salant figures are applied to this increase, we can estimate that about 20,000 workers were displaced by the 1956 tariff cuts.

The third study was made in 1952, when the United States government was still concerned with the inability of the European countries to earn enough to pay for their imports. Howard S. Piquet, the international trade expert at the Library of Congress, attempted to determine how much American imports might be increased by a complete elimination of tariffs. He made a product-by-product analysis covering four fifths of our dutiable imports. Adding up the results he concluded that imports might rise by from $1.2 to $2.6 billion.[6] Again applying Salant's figures, this would mean 124,000 to 268,000 workers losing jobs.

The complete elimination of tariffs is not generally contemplated today, but Piquet's figures are useful in showing the limited over-all impact of even such a radical move. Out of the total American labor force of over 70,000,000, less than 1 percent would be affected. The Kreinin estimates of the effect of the type of reductions which have actually been taking place in recent years run to only about 1 job for every 2,000 workers.

The total number of jobs which may be lost by future tariff reductions does not therefore loom large in our general economy, and, as we will note later, compensating employment increases are probable. But in specific industries the impact can be quite severe. There are pockets of serious unemployment in, for example, the glove industry in upper New York which are in considerable degree attributable to imports. From 70 to 80 percent of the American production of women's and children's leather dress gloves comes from the area centering around Gloversville and Johnstown, N.Y. This segment of the glove industry employs some 5,000 workers; 5,000 more are engaged in making other types of leather gloves. In 1961 unemployment in the Gloversville-Johnstown area was around 8 percent of the labor force. The glove industry's problems are due in part to changes in style. Women and children just don't wear leather dress gloves as much as they used to. But imports have hurt. After an exhaustive study, the National Planning Association concluded that complete exclusion of imports might increase income in the area by as much as 15 percent.[7]

The textile industry has a similar situation. For many years it has suffered from unemployment due to domestic problems. Now its difficulties have been aggravated by swelling imports, chiefly from Italy and the Orient. Imports of knit gloves have climbed till they meet 50 percent of our demand. The inflow of men's trousers reached 45 million pairs in 1960, about 20 percent of domestic production. Such statistics mean that American workers all along the chain of production, from spinning to cutting and sewing, lost jobs.

Thus, while the over-all impact of imports is small, in specific sectors of our economy they can hurt severely. Only around 25,000 jobs may be lost over a couple of years by tariff reductions. But those jobs will tend to be concentrated in a few localities. When even 1,000 workers are laid off in an area like Gloversville, which is heavily dependent upon one industry, there is real suffering. Men who have devoted their lives to learning the skilled work of glove-making cannot learn a new trade overnight. And people who have built their lives around a community do not readily pick up and move to a new area. One must weigh carefully, therefore, the cost in human and economic terms of the potential benefits of trade liberalization.

The Two-way Street of Trade

The logic of those who advocate reducing tariffs and quotas starts with the basis for trade itself. Eash unit in an economy specializes in some form of production in which it is relatively efficient, selling its output and buying from others. This is true of individuals, of companies, and of countries. It is essential to the high standard of modern living.

The classic example is the banana. A New Yorker could grow his own bananas in a large hothouse, but they would probably cost him several dollars a pound. By concentrating on things which he can produce more economically, exporting them, and buying bananas for fifteen cents a pound from the tropics, he is able to get much more out of his efforts.

This pattern of specialization, often referred to as the "theory of comparative advantage," makes the wheels of trade move and brings gains to all who participate in it — bananas for New Yorkers, machinery for Guatemalan banana growers, coffee for Detroiters, automobiles for Colombians, and so on. Its values are obvious in extreme cases like bananas and coffee. No one seriously proposes a protective tariff to permit New Yorkers to raise and sell bananas at a profit because it would clearly raise prices very high, to the disadvantage of the public.

To the advocate of free trade, this concept, if it is logical in theory and in the extreme cases, must be equally valid for any trading situation. He sees no fundamental difference between the lower cost of watchmaking in Switzerland and banana growing in Guatemala.

The advantage of Switzerland is lower wages than those in the United States and that of Guatemala, both climate and wages. But the result is the same — lower cost — and, if in each case we make a fair exchange by selling some export in which we have a cost advantage, there is the same sort of mutual profit in the trading.

The protectionists, on the other hand, see wage-cost advantages as something different. They accept variations in climate and distribution of raw materials as facts of nature beyond our control. But wage rates are a creation of man, and the generally lower level of wages abroad is something against which we must protect ourselves. They visualize a wave of low-cost imports forcing down domestic prices and wages and putting our manufacturers out of business.

Illustrated with vivid stories of unemployment and depressed wages in the watch, glove, and similar industries, this line of thinking has a realistic ring. It is inaccurate, however, because it is incomplete. It attempts to draw total conclusions from only one piece of a complex trading pattern and is no better, therefore, than the description of an elephant by a blind man who could only feel the trunk.

The fallacy of the fear of low foreign wages is indicated by the regular exchange of manufactured goods between high- and low-wage countries. There are certain regulators incorporated into our trading system which, while they do not work perfectly, on the whole keep the system in balance. They make it possible for high- and low-wage countries to benefit but not suffer from each other's comparative advantages.

To see how the system works, let us consider what would happen if Japan, with its low wages and well-developed industry, were able to offer all its manufactured goods at the existing exchange rate (of, say, 700 yen to 1 United States dollar) for prices from 10 to 80 percent below our domestic production. There would, of course, be a tremendous import volume of Japanese products and a negligible flow of American manufactures to Japan. There would be some American export of food and raw materials but, judging by current experience, it could not be enough to balance a completely one-sided flow of manufactured goods. Japan would therefore have a large export surplus and the United States a comparable deficit in its trade account. The imbalance might be covered for a while by dollar reserves, gold, or some other means. But it could not continue indefinitely because there are limits to such resources.

Thus a readjustment would have to be made, most likely by one or more of three means. First, our government might impose direct restrictions on imports, as many countries have in the postwar era. There is a general aversion now to such direct controls, however; hence reliance would more likely be placed on the other two methods.

Second, the fact that Japan was exporting much more than it was importing would result in a shortage of goods in the domestic Japanese market. The demand for the limited supply would push prices up. As prices became inflated they would become progressively less attractive to American importers. For example, we may assume that a woman's sweater was priced at 3,500 yen in Japan, equivalent to $5. Comparable sweaters made in the United States cost $6; hence the imported sweaters have sold well in the United States. But if inflation pushes the Japanese price up to 4,900 yen, the price in the United States will rise to $7 and imports will stop. Similar changes in price relations for a range of products would reduce Japanese exports and start a reverse flow of American exports to Japan, equalizing the trade.

Third, the excess of the demand for yen as compared with the demand for dollars would push the dollar price of yen up. Let us say that the value of Japanese exports was running at 700 million yen or $1 million per year against American exports of 350 million yen or $0.5 million. The $1 million offered by American importers would be competing to buy the 350 million yen available from American export earnings or only half enough to meet the need at the 700 to 1 exchange rate. The competitive bidding by the importers would force the price of the yen in dollars up until, let us say, it took $2 rather than $1 to buy 700 yen, or the exchange rate was 350 to 1. At this point, the price of Japanese products in United States dollars would have doubled. The Japanese sweater priced at 3,500 yen would cost $10 and be unable to compete with our sweaters priced at $6. Thus again the flow of imports into the United States would drop and that of exports would rise.

This, of course, is an extreme and highly simplified example, but the principles it illustrates are at work adjusting our trading relationships all the time. So far as wage differentials are concerned, the result is to permit the exportation by poor countries of those products in which their low wages give them the greatest comparative advantage while they import those products in which wages are least significant. As one might expect, these low-wage countries are most competitive in industries where labor requirements are high.

While, in general, labor costs are only 20 to 25 percent of sales prices for United States manufacturers, a study by Percy Bidwell points out that in the industries hit by import competition they run higher: 30 to 35 percent in woolens and worsteds, 60 percent in chinaware, 65 percent in hand-fashioned glassware, and 80 percent in watches.[8]

Who Benefits from Trade Liberalization?

With this picture of the whole system in mind, we can focus on the two beneficiaries of liberal trade policies: export industries and the general public. Each stands to gain as the system operates freely, permitting the importing of lower-cost goods and the export of products in which we have a cost advantage.

That exports should increase to offset any increase in imports follows logically as part of the system of adjustments just discussed. However, it is rarely demonstrable in the same dramatic manner as the losses suffered by domestic industries hit by import competition. The gains are likely to develop over time and to be diffused over many industries. We must rely, therefore, on the indirect evidence of the consistent growth of exports paralleling that of imports as shown in Figure 8. Supplementing this dollar data is an analysis by Franz Gehrels of the relation of employment to production volume

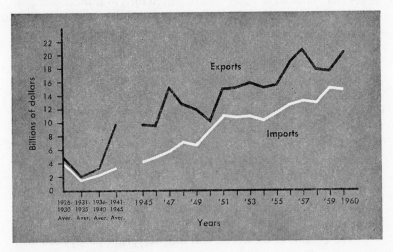

FIG. 8.   United States exports and imports.
Source: See Appendix, Table 1.

in export and import industries.[9] It shows that on the average 110 workers are replaced by each $1 million of imports and a like number of new jobs are created by a $1 million increase in export industries.

Some of this adjustment may be readily accomplished within industries. A number of our "import-injured" industries have a healthy export business in certain products based upon research or superior production efficiency. This is notably true of textiles and electrical machinery. Thus some workers can simply be shifted from one job to another in the same trade.

But the transfer of labor from one industry to another is more significant and beneficial because the import industries, such as textiles, have generally lower wages than the strong export industries, such as machinery. The average hourly earnings in the leather glove industry in 1961 were about $1.50 and in textiles about $1.65. In machine tool manufacturing the earnings averaged around $2.65 per hour. In a comprehensive analysis of all industries which suffer from appreciable import competition, Professor Irving Kravis of the University of Pennsylvania found that the hourly earnings of their workers averaged 10 percent below the general level of American industry and in some cases were 30 to 35 percent lower.[10] Thus, using Gehrels's figures, when we have equal increases of $1 million of imports and of exports, there is a good chance that 110 jobs on the lower end of our wage scales are exchanged for 110 at the higher end.

The prominence of high-wage industries in our export trade is worth noting as further evidence of the fallacy of the fear of low wages abroad. Low wages do not necessarily mean low total costs because they may be accompanied by other labor costs (family benefits, housing, and so on) and by low productivity which force total costs quite high. The high wages found in our export industries are indicative of the high productivity of their workers based upon technical skill, mechanized operations, and mass-production techniques. It is these qualities which give us our comparative trading advantage, and the higher wages of the workers are their share of the rewards of the beneficial trade. Conversely, the low wages in our less productive industries are one price we pay for continued reliance on domestic production which is comparatively less economical than imports.

The benefits of the free flow of imports for the public need little comment. Clearly, the man who can purchase a Hong Kong–made sports shirt for thirty cents less than a domestic one has thirty cents more with which to buy something else. Likewise, in those cases where prices are now held up by tariffs he is forced to pay more for the protected products and has less for other purchases. No one has computed the full cost to the American public of current tariffs, but we may gauge it roughly by the somewhat similar Canadian situation. As part of the government-sponsored Gordon Commission study of the Canadian economy, J. H. Young determined that the excess cost to consumers due to the tariff was "3.5 to 4.5% of gross national expenditure."[11] For a typical American earning around $5,000 a year, that means the elimination of tariffs would add about $200 of extra buying power per year.

The Pains of Progress

The fundamental advantages from liberal trade policies are evident. But their achievement is, and doubtless always will be, hindered by real problems of economic transition. Because the workings of free economies are finely balanced, there must always be a certain number of marginal industries, such as glovemaking, which live close to the brink, but surviving so precariously that any significant lowering of prices seriously jeopardizes their existence. As our dynamic society moves along there must inevitably be changes in the comparative advantages of nations, bringing some of these marginal industries under competitive pressure. If the pressures developed slowly, industry by industry, our economy might be adjusted to them fairly readily. But they tend rather to come in broad waves at particular moments, generating strong public pressure for protection.

This pattern can be seen well in the history of our tariffs shown in Figure 9. Each of the major rises is associated with a depression or a period of industrial stress often at the end of a rapid, wartime expansion that brought new, high-cost industries into being. The first Tariff Act in 1789 had relatively low rates averaging about 8.5 percent and was intended primarily as a source of revenue. During the European conflicts and the War of 1812, high-cost American factories for glass, textiles, and other consumer products mushroomed. With the coming of peace these industries suddenly faced stiff import competition and the protectionist Tariff Act of 1816 resulted, followed by further increases in 1824 and finally the "Tariff of Abominations" in 1828, with rates averaging around 50 percent. There followed a period in which the new industries gradually

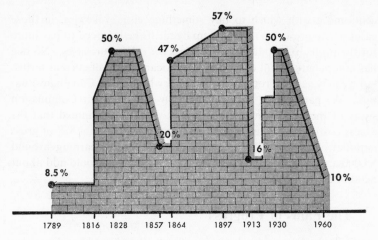

FIG. 9. Average tariff rates on dutiable imports. (Only the rates for which figures are shown are computed. Rates for intervening years are approximations to complete the illustration.)

established their competitive strength independent of protection, and tariffs were lowered, reaching about 20 percent by 1857.

Then came the Civil War with a need for more revenue and a new wave of industrial growth. The Southern cotton exporters, who had been the strongest voice for free trade, were submerged, and protection-minded industrialists supported new tariffs which reached an average rate of 47 percent by 1864. This general trend prevailed through the McKinley era, reaching a zenith in the Dingley Tariff of 1897, with rates averaging 57 percent. With the ascendancy of the Democrats, tariffs were lowered by the Underwood Act of 1913 to an average of 16 percent. But after World War I yet another set of competitive pressures appeared, this time against much of our agriculture and certain war-born industries. A new protectionist period started with the act of 1922 and was climaxed with the Smoot Hawley Tariff of 1930 with average rates of 50 percent in response to the distress of many domestic industries. The problems this time were primarily due to overexpansion and the start of the great depression, but industry and agriculture saw in the exclusion of imports some relief from their internal problems.

Under the Trade Agreements Act of 1934 rates have again been brought to a low level. But, as we look at the world economic situation, we can see the same sort of competitive stresses building up which in earlier periods have inaugurated periods of protection. At home, industry is burdened with overcapacity, unemployment is high, and the economy seems to lack the vitality to overcome its problems. Abroad, industrial expansion is strengthening the competitive position of a variety of manufactures, especially of consumer goods (Japanese radios, Italian knit goods, and so on). As mass markets develop, they are able to combine mass production with low wages, establishing a comparative advantage over American producers.

Looking at this situation calmly in a long-run perspective, we can see in it the basis for a mutually beneficial period of progress. As economies expand and incomes rise abroad, their need for some American exports decreases, but at the same time their demand for others increases, notably for our food surpluses and complex machinery and similar manufactures produced by high-wage labor. At the same time, their lower-cost consumer items are imported to the benefit of the American public.

A steady transition toward these benefits is essential both to economic welfare and to world peace. If we attempt to thwart it by erecting barriers to foreign products, we are almost certain to set off a sequence of retaliatory tariffs and other restrictions such as those that followed the enactment of the Smoot-Hawley Tariff in 1930. That world-wide reversion to nationalism added to the economic woes of the period and contributed to the animosities which led to World War II.

But, while we dare not check the course of economic progress, we cannot ignore its cost in the industries hit hard by import competition. As a matter of humanity as well as practical politics the problems of manufacturers and labor must be understood and dealt with effectively.

Easing the Pain

There are two basic approaches to solving these problems: regulating the increase in imports so that the transition is absorbed gradually, and helping the industries hurt by import competition.

The first approach has been in effective operation since the adoption of the Trade Agreements Act in 1934. Prior to that, tariff rates were determined by Congress and thus subject to large, unilateral changes at irregular intervals when new tariff acts were passed. The process was cumbersome and involved much political logrolling as legislators seized opportunities to gain protection for constituents in particular industries. Under the Trade Agreements Act, Congress delegated to the President the power to negotiate treaties with other countries reducing our tariffs in return for similar concessions. The act has been revised and renewed eleven times since then, most recently for four years in 1958. Despite the violent complaints of protectionists, the system as it has evolved does permit progress toward the benefits of liberal trade but at a gradual pace which prevents severe dislocations in import industries. The approach has two main facets: reciprocity and moderation.

The practice of obtaining reciprocal tariff reductions with other countries is intended to assure that for every increase in imports there shall be an opportunity for us to increase our exports. There can be no guarantee that the results are perfectly accomplished, but this does lay the basis for achievement of the over-all benefits of liberalized trade which might be frustrated by unilateral tariff reductions. At first, these reciprocal reductions were worked out in treaties with individual countries. Since 1947, however, they have been the product of multilateral negotiations under the General Agreement on Tariffs and Trade (GATT), including most of the nations of the free world. The members of GATT meet every three years. Negotiations take place between pairs of countries for reciprocal concessions, but as the concessions made by any nation are extended to all others under the "most favored nation" clause in the treaties, the result for practical purposes is a multilateral agreement.

The emergence of the European Common Market has created a need for some changes in our trade agreements program. The negotiations previously have been on a product-by-product basis. We will negotiate with the British to lower our bicycle tariff in return for a reduction in their duty on machine tools, for example. But the Common Market countries have negotiated their tariff arrangements on the basis of broad product groups — all types of machinery, textile products, and so forth. At the GATT negotiations in the fall of 1961, the EEC group offered a general 20 percent reduction in all tariffs. The United States negotiators were only able to propose reductions of varying percentages on a product-by-product basis. This divergence of policies severely cramped the negotiations and for a time it seemed possible that they would break down completely. Eventually agreement was reached in January, 1962, with the EEC, making across-the-board concessions and the United States varying reductions on a large number of individual products. This experience was ample demonstration that the United States must develop a new approach which will permit us to bargain for over-all reductions in our tariffs, not just product-by-product changes.

Moderation is built into the United States tariff program in several ways. First, in each extension of the Trade Agreements Act, Congress has limited the amount by which tariffs may be lowered. The 1958 extension, for example, provided that rates might be reduced by either 20 percent or 2 percentage points (e.g., from 7 to 5 percent duty) with not more than half of each reduction made in one year. It also permitted excessively high rates to be reduced to 50 percent, with not more than one third of the reduction in any one year. For example, a duty which had been 80 percent could be cut to 70 percent in one year, to 60 percent the next year, and, finally, to 50 percent after three years.

Second, under the "peril point" clause, limits are set to prevent serious injury to domestic industry. Before negotiations with other countries, all proposed concessions are the subject of hearings and analysis by the Tariff Commission, a relatively autonomous government agency. The commission determines the lowest level to which each rate may be dropped without causing serious injury. The President is not legally restricted by the peril-point determination, but it is a restraining influence in negotiations as an industry subject to a rate below the peril-point has a strong case in seeking future relief which would nullify any concessions. In fact, the President has kept concessions within the peril-point limits in thousands of individual negotiations, exceeding them in only two minor cases — tungsten alloys and violins and violas.

Third, since 1951 an "escape clause" must be incorporated into all trade agreements permitting the United States to withdraw any concessions if rate reductions cause serious injury to domestic industry. Application for relief under the escape clause is made to the Tariff Commission. If the commission, after holding hearings and studying the situation, determines that serious injury has been caused, it recommends an increase in rates to the President. The President may accept or reject the recommendations, the latter action being subject to reversal by a two-thirds majority in both houses of Congress.

The functioning of the escape clause can be seen in the story of the bicycle industry. The tariff on bicycles was set at 30 percent by the 1930 Tariff Act. In 1938, a reciprocal trade agreement was negotiated with Great Britain reducing the rate to 7.5 percent for some models and 15 percent for others. These rates were incorporated into the GATT agreement signed in 1948. In the immediate postwar years bicycle imports were moderate, but then the British began developing the United States market for their products actively. Imports rose from 8 percent of United States bicycle sales to a peak of 41 percent in 1955. Part of the loss of position by the American manufacturers was due to their slowness in offering light-weight models to compete with the superior British design. But the industry appealed to the Tariff Commission for relief and the commission agreed that imports were causing serious injury to the domestic producers. It recommended that the duty be increased by 50 percent under the escape clause and the President approved the increase in 1955. With the higher tariff and better product design the American industry was able to regain much of the lost ground, imports filling only 28 percent of the American demand in 1959.

The escape clause has been used sparingly. The Tariff Commission had recommended higher duties in only 31 of the 125 cases heard up to June 30, 1961. The President has approved the increases in only 13 of these cases. But the existence of the system provides another restraining influence against extreme changes.

Fourth, while not a formal part of the trade agreements program, one must note the acceptance of the concept of moderation by our trading partners. The notable example is the adoption by the Japanese of voluntary export quotas for textile products to limit the impact of their growing competitive strength on our own textile industry. There have been gradual increases in the quota permitting some growth of imports. The 1962 limit, for example, was set at 275 million square yards, 7 percent above that for 1961. But this is considerably less than the 30 percent increase desired by the Japanese exporters, which they could probably realize without the quota. Thus this restraint has greatly reduced the pressure from the textile industry for restrictions imposed by the United States government, restrictions which would have been a sharp setback for liberal trade policies.

In combination, these aspects of the system provide for a gradual adjustment in the direction of more liberal trade. They are frustrating to the advocates of free trade, who feel the progress toward their goal is unduly slow. They contend that the protection from "serious injury" is unsound because attainment of the benefits of trade requires the demise of industries in which we do not have comparative advantage. They draw a parallel with the fate of industries overrun by technological advance, observing that our economy would have been greatly retarded if, for example, the sales of automobiles had been checked to prevent serious injury to buggy-whip manufacturers. But the progress toward lower tariffs is real, and the steady increase of imports accompanied by declining employment in some industries indicates that the economic adjustments are being made even though their pace may have been slowed.

Quite naturally the protected industries have never been satisfied with the trade agreements program. Taking an objective view of the situation, however, we can say that they have been treated more kindly than private enterprise has a right to expect in a system based on free competition. A slowly declining tariff is for practical purposes the same as a graduated subsidy and permits the affected industries to adjust slowly to competition.

The regulation of the increase in imports has been relatively effective in the past but it has two important limitations in the current situation. First, United States tariffs have been reduced so effectively that few additional reductions can be made without causing "serious injury" to domestic industries. Second, the idea of across-the-board reductions negotiated with the Common Market countries does not permit the type of exceptions for specific industries which have been part of the peril-point system. Thus the major objectives sought by liberal trade advocates in 1962 are elimination of the "peril-point" limits and authority for across-the-board tariff cuts, regardless of injury to individual industries. Such a program cannot hope to win Congressional approval against protectionist forces, however, without some tangible solution for the injured industries' problem.

New interest has therefore been attracted to the second approach to easing the transition: direct help to affected industries. For the most part this approach has not progressed beyond the talking stage. A number of proposals have been made to give financial assistance to companies and communities, and retraining and other help for workers.[12]

The most widely considered proposal was made by David McDonald of the AFL-CIO when he was a member of the Randall Commission in 1954.[13] His proposal provided for assistance in a number of ways. The federal government would pay for the services of consulting engineers, market researchers, and other technicians employed by injured companies and communities in their efforts to convert to new types of production. Loans would be provided to finance new operations. Accelerated depreciation of plant and equipment would be allowed to ease the tax burden of new factories. And these companies and communities would receive special consideration in the assignment of government supply contracts.

For the affected workers, special unemployment compensation would be paid beyond the limits of regular programs. The federal government would provide counseling and placement services to locate alternative employment for them. Special retraining programs and moving allowances would be financed to help workers to shift to new jobs. For older workers who could not be relocated, early retirement privileges would be permitted with full eligibility for social security payments.

The Randall Commission expressed interest in Mr. McDonald's proposal and published it in the commission report. However, the group did not endorse it, stating: "In a free economy, some displacement of workers and some injury to institutions is unavoidable. It may come about through technological change, alterations in consumer preferences, exhaustion of a mineral resource, new inventions, new taxes, or many other causes. Since it has never been seriously proposed that the burden of all such injury arising in a free economy should be assumed by the Government, the Commission felt that it was not appropriate to propose such a plan in the tariff area only."

In 1961 the assistance idea appeared as a special section on areas affected by imports in S.1, the "Depressed Areas" bill, but this section also had lukewarm response. The slow progress of this approach is due in large part to the lack of support by the protectionists. While its provisions are intended to help them, they resist because approval would be tantamount to accepting the lowering of tariffs and the increase of imports, a proposition to which they will never accede. The Gloversville manufacturers want to keep on making gloves. Financial help in shifting their production to some new type of product is a highly undesirable alternative to them and so they will fight for protection to the end. Horace B. McCoy, President of the Trade Relations Council of the United States, a prominent protectionist lobbying organization, states their position concisely: "We would place a barrier at the top of the cliff. S.1

would put a hospital at the bottom."[14] Reinforcing the protectionists is a general aversion in industry and Congress to anything which smacks of direct subsidy. Among the advocates of free trade, the assistance concept does not win full support because it is contrary to the principles of free competition—no one helped the buggy-whip makers!

Until recently, therefore, this approach has had strong support only among labor groups. Now it seems to be gaining in popularity among the liberal trade policy group as the only practical way to make further gains toward their objectives. They cannot hope to win over the archprotectionists, but the idea is valuable in carrying their case to the public as a whole and to labor groups among whom there is increasing concern over import-induced unemployment. Thus the Kennedy administration has adopted the assistance concept as a major part of its trade policy proposals. In making his request for new tariff reduction authority for a five-year period from the 1962 Congress, President Kennedy specifically sought approval of aid for injured industries along the lines of the McDonald program.

A Continuing Struggle

The tariff issue will never be settled because there will always be weak industries pleading for protection and proponents of free trade advocating the benefits of exchanges among nations according to the laws of comparative advantage. But we have come a long way toward evolving a system to ease the pains of adjustment for industries hit by import competition while still furthering the growth of our stronger export industries and permitting increases of inexpensive imports for the good of the public. Our best hope lies in continuing and perfecting the trade agreements program with its slow, reciprocal reduction of tariffs and in developing effective methods of directly helping injured industries.

■■■■■■■■■■ *4*

Havens
from the
Harsh Tax Winds

"Tax haven" sounds like tax evasion. Tax evasion is evil. Q.E.D.: Tax havens must be bad.

This seems to be the essence of the tax-haven issue as it has filtered down to the public from the complex debates of the tax experts. The formal attack by the U.S. Treasury Department against tax-haven companies has included more refined criticisms, notably that these companies foster foreign investment in preference to domestic development and that their practices amount to using interest-free government loans for investment. But the heart of the issue rests upon the argument that tax-haven companies are a device to defer payment of taxes to which the United States government has a rightful immediate claim. Prompted by the balance of payments crisis, the Treasury is pressing for elimination of what it describes as the "privilege" of tax deferral.

The Origin of the Issue

At the root of this matter is the widespread practice among United States firms of financing overseas operations from retained profits of foreign operations channeled through so-called tax-haven countries. New capital sent out from the United States has provided the largest portion of the money needed for expansion abroad, especially by companies which have only recently entered international business. But companies with established overseas subsidiaries have been retaining a big share of their foreign profits and plowing them back into expansion abroad. For example, while International Harvester had profits of $15 million in 1960 from its 35 overseas farm equipment plants and sales units, the parent company received only $10 million of dividends. The remaining $5 million was put into new production facilities overseas. The aggregate effect of similar reinvestments by many companies is shown in Figure 10. Of the $13.4 billion of new investments in the five years

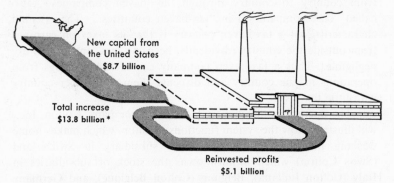

New capital from
the United States
$8.7 billion

Total increase
$13.8 billion *

Reinvested profits
$5.1 billion

*The net change in investments between 1956 and 1960 was $13.4 billion. The difference between this and the $13.8 for new investments is due to changes in asset valuations, expropriations, etc.

FIG. 10. Financing of new United States investments abroad, 1956 - 1960.
Source: Survey of Current Business, U. S. Department of Commerce.

from 1956 to 1960, $5.1 billion or about 40 percent came from profits retained abroad.

While reinvestment of profits is partly a matter of convenience, it is economically beneficial because it minimizes the United States tax payments. The $10 million of dividends that International Harvester received from abroad were subject to the United States corporate income tax of 52 percent. The company received a credit for the foreign taxes which had already been paid on the income of the subsidiaries so it did not have to pay the full 52 percent.[1] But since corporate income taxes in most countries are lower than ours, the company loses some of its foreign income to the United States taxes when it brings the dividends home. The differences are not great in Canada and Europe, which receive the bulk of our investment. But there is some loss in virtually all cases. If the additional $5 million had been brought home by International Harvester as dividends and a comparable sum sent out as new capital, some money would therefore have been lost to the United States taxes. Thus by simply keeping the $5 million abroad beyond the reach of the U.S. Treasury, International Harvester gets the most out of its money.

In its simplest form, this practice merely involves the use of profits in one country to expand operations in that same country. Most interest, however, has centered around the shifting of profits from country to country through "tax-haven companies" (also called "base companies") in "tax-haven countries." The essential characteristic of a tax-haven country is that its taxes on earnings from outside the country (dividends, licensing fees, and so on) are negligible. Thus a tax-haven company can receive earnings from operations in one country and dispense them to another country with little tax loss.

The operations of a fictional American company, Colton, Inc., will illustrate how the system functions. Colton, which makes home washing machines, has a tax-haven subsidiary in Switzerland (Swiss Colton) which in turn owns the stock of subsidiaries in Italy (Colton Italiana), Belgium (Colton Belgique), and Germany (Colton GmbH). The taxes in Switzerland vary among the cantons (states), and Swiss Colton is located in a canton where the combined (federal and canton) taxes on foreign dividends are 5 percent. The company is currently making good profits in Italy which it is using to expand the Belgian factory (Figure 11). On $100,000 of profits Colton Italiana pays a 31 percent Italian income tax, so $69,000 of dividends is available to Swiss Colton. The Swiss taxes of 5 percent cost Swiss Colton another $3,450, and the remaining $65,550 is invested in Colton Belgique. If the money had been routed from Colton Italiana through Colton, Inc., the amount collected by the United States government, after tax credit computations, would have been $14,500, leaving only $54,500 for investment in Belgium. The United States taxes might have been avoided by a loan from Colton Italiana to Colton Belgique or by some other device, but the Swiss tax-haven company system is considered the most flexible and convenient arrangement.

There is nothing new about the tax-haven concept. A few companies were using tax-havens before World War II. However, with the great expansion of our international business and the high level of United States taxes, they have mushroomed tremendously in the past decade. A survey by the National Industrial Conference

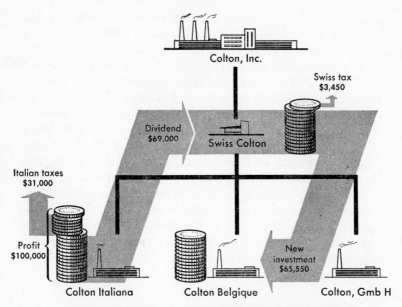

FIG. 11.   Financing a new investment through a tax haven.

Board of a sample of American companies operating abroad revealed that one third had tax-haven companies, 80 percent of them formed since 1955.[2] The Treasury estimated that over 500 American corporations were established in Switzerland by March 31, 1961, 170 of them created in the previous year,[3] and a host of base companies are to be found in the other popular tax-haven countries: the Bahamas, Liberia, Liechtenstein, Panama, and Venezuela.

Up to a year or so ago, the general principle of American companies expanding overseas operations in this manner was supported as part of our basic program to foster foreign economic growth. However, the Kennedy administration has taken a sharply different tack, prompted chiefly by the balance of payments situation, which we will observe in the next chapter, along with a desire to capture more tax revenue. Retained overseas earnings running around $1 billion per year (as shown in Table 5 in the Appendix) looked very promising to Treasury officials confronted with a large budget deficit and a 1960 balance of payments deficit in which the outflow of dollars exceeded the inflow by $3.8 billion.

In the spring of 1961 President Kennedy proposed that all

profits retained in developed countries or in tax havens be subject to United States taxes. Secretary of Treasury Dillon estimated that this would result in improvement in our balance of payments position by as much as $390 million per year and increased tax revenue of $250 million.[4] The Ways and Means Committee of the House of Representatives rejected the taxation of profits retained in developed countries and advised the Treasury to draft a bill covering tax-haven operations only, these being the main concern of the government.

The new Treasury draft proposed that American overseas subsidiaries be subject to United States taxes on their profits from "tax-haven transactions," (defined as purchase and resale of exports to other countries, commissions as an agent for such transactions, licensing and servicing fees, dividends from subsidiaries in other countries, and insurance fees.) The result, for practical purposes, would be to tax the retained profits of a company like Swiss Colton as though it were a domestic American corporation, with allowance of a credit for such foreign taxes as had been paid.

Rights and Principles

The debate about tax-haven companies revolves around two major questions: first, whether the United States government is legally or administratively in a position to tax their profits before these are transferred to their parent companies in the United States and, second, whether the balance of payments situation requires rigorous corrective actions, of which this is one possibility. The second question, which calls for examination of the whole balance of payments subject, is covered in the next chapter. Here I will deal only with the first question, which is essentially whether the United States has a legitimate right to tax the profits of tax-haven companies and, to the extent that it does, whether it is practical to enforce its claim.

To reach conclusions on these points we must look at the operations of a tax-haven company such as Swiss Colton in the context of existing law. Swiss Colton is a *corporation* chartered in a *foreign country* and owned by a *United States stockholder*, Colton, Inc. Under generally accepted legal concepts these three characteristics have certain quite clear-cut results:

First, because the corporation is *foreign* it is outside the normal jurisdiction of the United States government, its laws, its powers of taxation, and its courts. This is a basic part of the mutual respect for national sovereignty which has evolved over the centuries. There are legal situations, such as antitrust cases, where the interests of one nation are so affected by the actions of corporations in another country that the principles of sovereignty are strained. But any attempt of one nation to exercise jurisdiction over foreign companies must make a very strong case of vital national interest both in United States and foreign courts.

In the case of taxation, there is no precedent for claiming jurisdiction over profits earned abroad by a broad category of foreign corporations. The United States does tax the profits which foreign companies earn here. For example, it collects taxes from Shell Oil Company for the profits the British-Dutch company makes on the refining and sales operations it conducts in this country. But this is consistent with the general practice among governments of taxing profits where they are earned. As a *foreign* corporation, therefore, Swiss Colton is properly beyond the *direct* jurisdiction of the United States government because it does not earn profits in the United States.

Second, *shareholders* may be taxed only on the profits of a *corporation* as they are received in the form of dividends. One of the most fundamental legal concepts in our society is that of the "corporate individual." Corporations are considered legal entities distinct from their stockholders. General Motors, for example, functions in legal and business matters as an individual body quite clearly distinguished from its 830,000 stockholders. The person who owns GM stock is not legally obligated by the actions of General Motors, and the financial affairs of the corporation are clearly separated from his. The profits which General Motors made in 1960 amounted to about $3.35 on each of his shares of stock. But he had to pay income tax only on the $2.00 per share which was paid out in dividends. The remaining $1.35 was kept inside the corporate body of GM. The stockholder might eventually benefit from its reinvestment in the company, but the government has no right to tax him for it until he receives the benefits either through dividends or by selling his stock for a profit.

A corporation which owns the stock of a subsidiary corporation is legally in the same position as the GM stockholder. The government has no right, therefore, to make it pay taxes on the retained earnings of the subsidiary. Some confusion on this point arises because it is common practice for American companies, such as General Motors, to consolidate their accounts with those of their domestic subsidiaries, paying a combined tax. They do this, however, *at their own volition* because, as a practical matter, the domestic subsidiaries are subject to the same taxes and there are certain advantages in consolidating the accounts.

But a company in the position of Colton, Inc., is under no obligation to consolidate its accounts with those of Swiss Colton. As a shareholder it stands apart from the profits of the Swiss subsidiary (just as the GM stockholder is distinct from General Motors profits), and it is liable for United States taxes only upon the dividends Swiss Colton pays. The United States government cannot, therefore, properly claim a right to tax the retained earnings of tax-haven companies through the *indirect* route of sovereignty over the parent corporation.

These fundamental legal aspects of the situation do more than challenge the right of the United States to tax the overseas earnings of tax-haven companies. They also make it doubtful if such a tax law could be enforced. To enforce a tax law effectively our revenue service must be able to inspect the accounts of taxpayers and take them to court if they do not pay their taxes. So long as it is operating within the jurisdiction of our government its position is strong. However, collecting taxes from companies in a foreign country is another matter. It is practical only with the cooperation of the local government.

It seems quite likely that the governments of tax-haven countries would not cooperate with the United States government in this respect, especially Switzerland, which probably has the largest number of base companies. In this age of strong governments and extensive reporting of business accounts, the Swiss are something of an oddity. They cling to an individualistic, secretive pattern of business affairs in which the powers of government over the individual are held rigorously in check. The most notable manifestation of these attitudes is the Swiss bank-secrecy law under which a bank is forbidden to disclose information on depositor accounts to anybody, including the government, except in certain criminal cases, and then only by court order.

The Swiss are also vigorous protectors of the concepts of sovereignty, and one can predict with reasonable certainty that an attempt by the United States government to assert a right to tax

American subsidiaries, such as Swiss Colton, would meet a cold response. Thus our revenue agents would probably be trying to collect taxes from Swiss companies without the cooperation of either the Swiss government or its courts. The result would be that the honest companies would pay the taxes and the rest would slip by. The United States government might try to collect the taxes through its power over the parent corporations, but without legal access to the tax-haven company accounts it is hard to see how it could equitably enforce the law.

Who Earned the Profits?

The Treasury proposal to tax all tax-haven profits appears, therefore, to be neither legally proper nor administratively feasible. But there is an area in the tax-haven field in which the Treasury does have the rights on its side and in which it may hope to achieve at least part of its objectives. To understand this part of the story we must take a further look at the activities of Swiss Colton.

The activities we discussed earlier are essentially those of a holding company: owning the stock of subsidiaries, receiving dividends from some of them, and dispensing them for new investments in others. Under the principles of corporate identity and national sovereignty, the legitimacy of these activities cannot be questioned and they are beyond the reach of United States taxation.

However, Swiss Colton also engages in other activities which are more complex and raise questions of legitimacy. These activities include buying and selling Colton products, receiving fees for licensing of Colton patents to the European subsidiaries, and making various insurance and financial arrangements. Swiss Colton, in fact, is a funnel through which all commercial and financial business is channeled by the Colton management. The objective is to siphon off as much of the profits as possible in Switzerland, where the taxes are lowest, and to use these profits for new investments.

One of the most profitable phases of this activity has been the export of parts to the subsidiaries, especially to Colton GmbH. The German plant is equipped to manufacture the outside box of the washing machines and a number of the simpler internal parts. But the timing device which governs the washing cycle and several other precision components are made only in the Colton plant in

Ohio. In 1961, the components supplied for use in Germany had a factory cost to Colton, Inc., of $200,000. The company normally figures that the factory operations should earn 10 percent profit, so $20,000 would be a reasonable markup for these exports for use in Germany. However, Colton, Inc., instead charged only a nominal 3 percent profit and sold the washer components for $206,000 to Swiss Colton, as shown in Figure 12. The shipping and insurance costs added another $2,000.

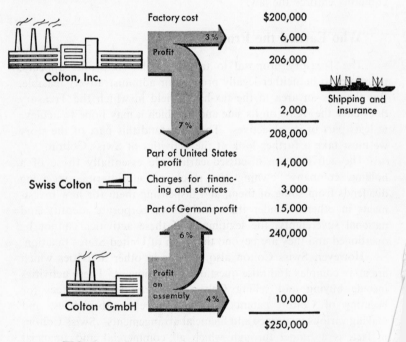

Factory cost	$200,000
Profit 3%	6,000
	206,000
Shipping and insurance	2,000
7%	208,000
Part of United States profit	14,000
Charges for financing and services	3,000
Part of German profit	15,000
6%	240,000
Profit on assembly 4%	10,000
	$250,000

FIG. 12. Payments of washer parts shipped to Germany.

The washer components were shipped directly to Colton GmbH but Swiss Colton made all the shipping and insurance arrangemen and owned the goods from the time they were packed in Ohio t they were received in Germany. The Swiss company charged percent interest for the two months while the goods were in tran and it also added a small profit for performing its other functi as a return on the investment in personnel and office equipr needed in Switzerland to make shipping and other arrangem

These charges, plus the actual expenses incurred by Swiss Colton, added up to $3,000 in 1961.

The price at which Swiss Colton sells the washer parts to Colton GmbH is determined by the German firm's income. Colton GmbH was able to sell its 1961 production of washing machines at prices which gave it a gross income of $500,000. It figured that the timers and other American components accounted for about half the value of the finished washing machines, or about $250,000 and it could reasonably figure a profit of about 10 percent, or $25,000, for them. However, the Colton management was anxious to minimize earnings in Germany because the German tax on retained profits was 51 percent. Therefore, only $10,000 of profits was allocated to Colton GmbH, and Swiss Colton was paid $240,000 for the parts.

As a result of these transactions, Swiss Colton ended up with a profit of $32,000, composed of $14,000 which Colton, Inc., might have charged as manufacturing profit on the exports, $3,000 for its own services, and $15,000 which Colton GmbH might have earned on its assembly and sales operations. There was substantial immediate gain because the first and third of these types of profit would have been subject to 52 and 51 percent tax respectively. Now only the 5 percent Swiss taxes must be paid so long as the profits are not paid out as dividends to Colton, Inc.

Variations of this pattern are used not only for sales of goods but also to channel into tax-haven companies income from patent licenses, management services, and other functions. The extent to which profits are diverted into tax-haven companies in this manner is not known because of the secrecy which shrouds their operations. It seems likely that such practices are widespread, though doubtless few companies go to the extremes employed by Colton. But, regardless of the degree, any distortion in allocation of profit raises questions. Of the three types of profits described in the Colton case, only the second — the $3,000 for interest and services — can be considered legitimately earned by Swiss Colton. The United States government can reasonably claim that it is entitled to tax the first type because it was the result of manufacturing effort within its jurisdiction and the German government has a similar claim on the third type.

In his Congressional testimony, Secretary Douglas Dillon cited this sort of situation as one of the major arguments for the Treasury proposals. However, taxation of all tax-haven company profits to correct the problem is using a shotgun where a rifle is needed. Mr. Dillon discussed the diversion of German profits as though this were a loss to us. Actually it is a source of ultimate gain to the U.S. Treasury since, when the tax-haven company eventually transmits the excess earnings to the United States as a dividend, they will be fully taxable. If the Germans had assessed their rightful tax of 51 percent on the $15,000 diverted to Swiss Colton, $7,650 less would have been available for future dividends and Colton, Inc., would receive a credit for the German tax so that the United States government would receive little or no tax. As matters stand, only 5 percent of the $15,000 will be lost and, when a dividend is eventually paid, the United States will collect some $6,700 of taxes. But the more important point is that this is none of our concern anyway. It is strictly a question between the Swiss and Germans.

We also have no right to tax the $3,000 of profits legitimately earned by Swiss Colton.

So that leaves only the $14,000 of profits which the American parent, Colton, Inc., should have made on its exports and we do not actually need new legislation to claim the taxes on them. The existing United States laws give our government the right to revise the accounts of any company so that they will show profits which have actually been earned. This power is already used in a variety of situations, such as the allocation of depreciation charges, and it is quite properly applicable to the tax-haven problem.

The difficulty is in enforcement, and herein lies the real root of the Treasury problem. In order to determine the true profits on the American exports, the revenue agents would have to examine the books of the tax-haven companies. But, as we have already seen, this requires cooperation from Swiss, Panamanian, and other tax-haven country officials who are none too enthusiastic about helping our Treasury at the expense of companies whom they are happy to have as residents.

Practical Solutions

Here, then, is a really knotty problem. The shotgun approach of the Treasury proposals seems highly inappropriate because it would not tax the right profits and, in violating the principle of sovereignty, would offend foreign governments, reducing the chances of gaining their cooperation. There appear to be only two possible solutions.

Neither will probably be fully effective but at least they offer some promise.

The simplest approach is to adopt new legislation which would result in more effective enforcement of our existing regulations. Specifically, a law could be passed which spelled out precisely the types of transactions in which the United States was losing rightful revenue and proposing reciprocal agreements with other governments for the enforcement of taxes against losses through improper allocations of profit. This would give our revenue agents a helpful assist in obtaining the cooperation abroad which is the critical element without which success cannot be achieved.

The second approach is the Foreign Business Corporation proposed in a bill written by Representative Hale Boggs which has been before Congress for several years. The Foreign Business Corporation would be a United States corporation entitled to receive profits from foreign subsidiaries and branches without paying taxes until it transmitted them to its stockholders as dividends. Thus, Colton, Inc., might set up Colton International, Inc., to perform the same functions as Swiss Colton. It would be, in effect, a United States-based tax-haven company. As even the best foreign tax havens involve risks and extra costs, most companies would probably shift their tax-haven activities to the new type of American corporation. This in itself would, of course, accomplish much of the balance of payments results which are a major reason for the attack on the tax havens. So far as checking illegitimate allocations of profit, the advantage would lie in bringing operations under the direct jurisdiction of our government. It is, of course, possible that some companies might prefer to continue to use overseas base companies for just this reason if their practices were questionable. However, companies doing business in a proper manner would probably prefer to operate from the American base, and the task of ferreting out offenders abroad would be simplified if their numbers were greatly reduced.

The Boggs bill never had the full support of the Eisenhower administration and today it is actively opposed by the Treasury, which is set on taxing all possible profits. The opposition in the Eisenhower period was on the ground that tax deferral for one type of corporation opens the door to claims for special tax concessions for all sorts of industries. It is hard to criticize this position because it rests on solid principles. Yet the Boggs proposal seems to be a sound and sensible adjustment to the realities of the current world situation. We have seen that elimination of the tax havens is not feasible. Would it not be better to bring the activities back here where they can operate under the supervision of our own government? The persuasiveness of this line of reasoning is indicated by the fact that the British have set up an overseas trade corporation with provisions similar to the Boggs proposal.

Questions of Equity

There remains one further criticism of tax havens to be considered. This is outside the fundamental legal and administrative aspects upon which the matter should be judged. But because it was raised by Secretary Dillon in his Congressional testimony, it requires comment. The essence of his position was stated as follows:

> With the present deferral privilege, an American firm contemplating a new investment and finding cost and market conditions comparable at home and abroad is impelled towards the investment opportunity overseas. This is so because it would thereafter be able to finance expansion on the basis of an interest-free loan from the U.S. Treasury, repayable at the option of the borrower.[5]

The "interest-free loan" idea is part of the basic Treasury argument that the United States government has a right to tax the profits of tax-haven companies. Following this line of reasoning, Treasury officials feel that a company like Swiss Colton already owes our government taxes on its retained earnings and the amount of these "deferred taxes" is in effect an interest-free loan from the Treasury. The basic assumption of this argument has already been discussed, so we need not pursue it. Since the government's claim to a right to tax the earnings is weak, then the deferred taxes should not be stigmatized in these terms.

But this still leaves one aspect of Secretary Dillon's comment which we should explore. As he indicates, the existence of the tax-haven system affects the relative merits of investments at home and abroad. There are many people who feel that the economics of using tax havens provide added incentives for overseas investment which has been detrimental to our domestic economy. The mathematics of base company investment systems provide support for this contention. Let us compare the results from $1,000 investments by Colton, Inc., in the United States and through Swiss Colton in other countries whose average taxes result in a combined rate of, say, 30 percent. In the first year each earns 10 percent or $100. In the United States, $52 goes for taxes and $48 is available for reinvestment. Abroad only $30 in taxes is paid and $70 may be reinvested. Thus after one year, the $1,000 investment has grown to $1,048 for Colton, Inc., and $1,070 for Swiss Colton. If this process is continued for four years, the American investment will have grown to $1,207 and that of the tax-haven company to $1,311. If at this point Swiss Colton pays the full $311 accumulated earnings to the parent, Colton, Inc., as a dividend, we find — after payment of United States taxes with credit for the foreign taxes paid — that the net gain is $242 compared with the $207 gained in the United States. Thus, there has been roughly a 20 percent advantage as a result of avoiding a part of the annual tax take-off of 52 percent for each annual cycle of reinvestment.

The potential financial advantage is thus indisputable. It is not, however, possible to jump immediately to the conclusion that this has been a significant factor in decisions by companies like Colton to invest abroad rather than at home. On the financial side a variety of considerations enters into investment decisions and, because of the greater risk involved abroad, foreign investments must typically show a higher profit potential. A 20 percent differential created by lower foreign taxes would probably do no more than put foreign and domestic investments on an even footing. And it must be emphasized that the 30 percent tax rate used in the example is on the low side. Tax rates in most substantial European countries, except Belgium with 28.5 percent, are higher (Germany 51, France 50, and Denmark 44 percent).

But the financial considerations are secondary to a company's size-up of the marketing-manufacturing situation. The fact that American investment has been increasing more rapidly abroad than at home is primarily the result of differences in rates of economic growth, especially in the case of Europe. As we noted in Chapter 2, European industry has been straining at the limits of its capacity to fill demand while that of the United States has been limping along well below full capacity.

Companies like Colton have been fighting a tough competitive battle in the United States with a saturated market for home appliances and a sluggish economy punctuated by periodic recessions. Europe, on the other hand, is in the midst of a continuing middle-class consumer boom in which a large portion of the population is suddenly finding itself able to buy many products, including home appliances, which it never could afford before. In Colton's case, for example, 62 percent of American homes already have washing machines, which is a high percentage of the potential, considering the number of families living in apartments and other situations where they are unlikely to want a machine. Annual sales of washers in 1959 and 1960 in the United States were actually lower than in 1955. By contrast, only about 25 percent of German homes now have washers and sales have been climbing steadily.

Thus the marketing-manufacturing strategy of company after company has called for expansion in Europe while a reduced rate of investment at home has been sufficient to keep pace with the slow growth of demand. It is this type of analysis, far more than any tax considerations, which has caused the heavy flow of new investment abroad. The tax havens are not a cause, but rather a mechanism that has been used to make the most of investments justified on more fundamental grounds.

An Unhappy Dilemma

The tax-haven situation is a source of embarrassment and frustration to the United States. The retention of earnings overseas undoubtedly worsens our immediate balance of payments position and the potential tax savings have encouraged companies to employ profit allocation systems which, to varying degrees, defer payment of taxes our Treasury might collect today. Yet under fundamental legal principles, most of the activities are legitimate and beyond the reach of the proper authority of our government. Furthermore, the assertion of even our legitimate rights in the collection of taxes on American profits which have been allocated to tax-haven companies is frustrated by the limits of sovereignty and by the lack of co-operation by foreign courts. The Treasury's attempt to tax all profits from tax-haven transactions is both legally unsound and administratively unrealistic. Our best course lies in reinforcing our existing regulations or in adopting the Boggs proposals which, while outside the usual tax concepts, would eliminate much of the embarrassment and frustration by bringing the tax-haven companies home.

■■■■■■■■■■■ *5*

Our
Unbalance
of Payments

In the four years from 1958 through 1961, American expenditures abroad exceeded receipts from other countries by $12.6 billion.

This is an appalling state of affairs. It means that as a nation we have been spending far beyond our income. An individual who ran his affairs that way would soon be in the poorhouse. For nations the compulsions to live within one's income are not the same as those for an individual. But they are there nonetheless, and the United States must bring its balance of international payments into line, or sooner or later it will come to the end of its resources.

The Changing Times

The major deficits in our international balance of payments have come as a rude shock to the United States. In the years immediately following World War II we looked with sympathy upon the rest of the world suffering from the "dollar gap." Very few countries seemed able to earn enough dollars to pay for the goods they wanted to buy from us. Our receipts from the rest of the world usually exceeded our expenditures, with a peak surplus of $4.8 billion in 1947. (See Appendix, Table 6, for a historical summary of the balance of payments.) In the mid-1950's, we had deficits in our balance of payments for several years, but the amounts never seemed worrisome. In fact, they had the beneficial effect of building up the financial reserves of foreign countries which had been dangerously low. As recently as 1957 there was a payments surplus of $500 million.

Then suddenly, in 1958, the tide turned and for four successive years we have had deficits of truly alarming magnitude. Our balance of payments, once the concern only of the small community of international specialists, has become a major national issue, reported on the front pages of newspapers and discussed throughout the land.

A great variety of solutions have been advanced to solve our problem, ranging from expanding exports and enticing more tourists from abroad to restricting imports and slashing foreign-aid expenditures. There is no doubt that the condition of our international payments is unhealthy and remedies are called for. But the medicines being offered to us are of very mixed quality. Some look promising but others seem quite capable of killing the patient in the process of curing the disease.

The Total Picture

As a starting point for considering this problem, we had best look at the over-all composition of our international transactions. The net effects of the various items which make up our balance of payments are shown in Figure 13 for 1960. A few of the figures

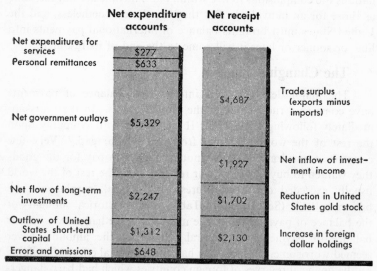

FIG. 13.   United States balance of payments summary for 1960 (in millions of dollars).
Source: Survey of Current Business.

stand out: notably the substantial surplus of exports over imports, the large investment earnings, and the major outflows for government expenditures, long-term investments, and short-term capital. These over-all figures are helpful in pointing out areas in which significant changes might be made. But there are many ins and outs for every item. Hence we must look carefully at each to determine just where our effort to improve the balance of payments should be directed.

Our Trade Balance

Over the years, our trading activities, shown in Figure 14, have been a consistent source of net earnings for the United States. Although we import large volumes of goods, we have always been able to sell even more to the rest of the world. On the import side we need a variety of raw materials, such as tin and rubber. We also must import foods, such as coffee and bananas, which we do not produce and others, such as sugar, in which our national production is deficient. And there is a considerable inflow of manufactured

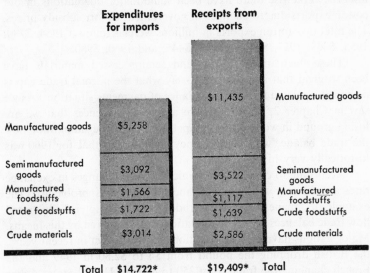

Expenditures for imports		Receipts from exports	
			Manufactured goods — $11,435
Manufactured goods	$5,258		
Semimanufactured goods	$3,092	$3,522	Semimanufactured goods
Manufactured foodstuffs	$1,566	$1,117	Manufactured foodstuffs
Crude foodstuffs	$1,722	$1,639	Crude foodstuffs
Crude materials	$3,014	$2,586	Crude materials
Total	$14,722*	$19,409*	Total

*The totals of the five items in each column are $14,652 and $20,990, respectively. The differences between these totals and the official totals of $14,772 for imports and $19,409 for exports are due to differences in methods of compiling the two sets of statistics.

FIG. 14. United States trade account for 1960 (in millions of dollars).
Source: Appendix, Table 1.

goods for which foreign costs are lower than ours: portable type-writers, bicycles, woolens, and the like.

But the physical wealth of our country has permitted a vastly greater volume of exports. Our productive land generates large surpluses of cotton, grain, iron and steel, and other basic products which other nations need. And our diversified and efficient manufacturing industries are able to sell machinery, chemicals, and other finished goods abroad, adding up to over twice the value of our imports in the same classification.

The size of our trade surplus has varied greatly during the past decade. In 1957, it reached a high point of $6.1 billion and in 1959 dropped to a postwar low of $1.0 billion. These major fluctuations have been caused by temporary changes in trading conditions. For example, the surge in 1956 and 1957 was largely due to the Suez crisis and the boom in Europe, which brought a heavy demand for petroleum, coal, and steel. In 1959 this demand tapered off at the same time that the steel strike cut our steel exports and stimulated imports. Likewise there have been some major fluctuations in our cotton exports due to changes in government export subsidy prices. The total raw cotton exports in millions were as follows: 1954, $780; 1955, $469; 1957, $1,049; 1959, $445; and 1960, $980.

These fluctuations in raw and semiprocessed materials have been so great that it is difficult to say what the normal trade gap is or how it is related to the total balance of payments situation. As we saw in Chapter 2, however, there are other evidences that we are losing ground in world trade competition; hence we should not view the trade balance with complacency even though that for 1960 was historically very high.

According to classical economic doctrines, changes in exchange rates are the way to correct balance of payments problems. The example of Japanese-American trade given in Chapter 3 illustrated how trade balances between two nations can be altered by this means. Major nations have used devaluations to good effect in recent years, the British dropping the pound from $4 to $2.80 in 1949 and the French changing the franc from 350 to 490 per United States dollar in 1957 and 1958. In both instances exports were stimulated and the countries' balance of payments situation improved.

A devaluation of the dollar would be accomplished by raising the dollar price of gold from its present $35 per ounce to, say, $40 or $50. If its effects could be restricted to our exports and imports, such a move might be desirable. However, few responsible people advocate a revaluation of the dollar at this time because its repercussions would go far beyond the trade area and would probably cause considerable damage to the whole world financial structure. The key factor is the status of the dollar as an international currency and the importance of maintaining confidence in it. This whole subject will be discussed in the next chapter. Suffice it at this point to say that a devaluation of the dollar would cause such disruption to the stability of international financial relations that it can be considered only as a last resort after all other ways of correcting our deficits have been exhausted.

Furthermore, there is a good chance that even the desired stimulus to exports would not be accomplished because many governments would probably immediately revalue their own currencies to maintain the current dollar exchange rates. This happened in the 1930's when the dollar was revalued by raising the price of gold from $21 per ounce to $35. Our move was followed by a wave of comparable revaluations by other nations.

Thus devaluation of the dollar seems virtually out of the question. There is, however, some possibility of alleviating the situation by adjustments of the exchange rates of other countries whose currencies do not have the same international role. In March, 1961, the Germans raised the value of the mark by 5 percent and this to a limited extent had the same effect as a 5 percent devaluation of the dollar. That is, it resulted in a 5 percent increase in German export prices and thus in the same relative price change in competition with American exports as a comparable United States devaluation. The impact was small, but considering that the Germans are one of our toughest competitors it was a beneficial boost to our payments situation. An American lathe, for example, which had been priced about 5 percent above a competing German machine would be put on an equal basis by the revaluation. In a number of selling situations the balance would be tipped toward American products with a resultant gain for our exports. It seems quite possible that there may be room for similar adjustments in the future which we can properly encourage as an aid to our balance of payments problem.

Setting aside devaluation of the dollar as impractical, our own actions must be confined to direct efforts to increase exports or decrease imports. The subject of export expansion was covered in Chapter 2. It need only be noted here that of the range of possible actions it is one of the most positive and constructive. Although the lag in exports has not apparently been a major cause of our predicament, still, if we can raise exports, it is a highly desirable way out of the deficit situation.

Throughout much of the free world import restrictions have become an accepted device for dealing with balance of payments difficulties. They are clearly a direct and simple corrective. And they would, of course, command strong support from the protectionist group, who could readily fill the domestic demand for a number of imported products — petroleum, textiles, and so on — though, of course, at a cost in higher prices to consumers.

But cutting back imports either by tariffs or quotas would be such a blow to the efforts to liberalize trade that it should be considered a last resort. The general nature of this problem was covered in Chapter 3 in considering the tariff question. Our balance of payments problem might be accepted to some degree by other countries as a legitimate excuse for checking imports. Still it could not help having a serious impact on many countries, such as Japan, for whom exports to the United States are a major source of income. It is quite probable, therefore, that, however understanding of our problems other countries might be, they would be forced to counter with restrictions against our exports to them. A wave of retaliatory restrictions would be a major setback to world trade and certainly to our exports. Thus any move to solve the deficit by reducing imports seems likely to boomerang.

Services and Private Remissions

The services and private remissions shown in Figure 15 do not loom large in our balance of payments, and for the most part the chances of decreasing our deficit through them are small.

Transportation expenses and receipts, which each run close to $2 billion per year, are primarily for shipping. The United States has been a net purchaser of shipping services for many years because of the high cost of our merchant marine. Building a ship involves a great deal of labor with little opportunity to use mass-production methods; hence it is just the type of industry in which foreign countries with lower wages have a large advantage over the United States. By the same token, sailing a ship takes many men and, with no notable superiority in the efficiency of its sailors, our merchant

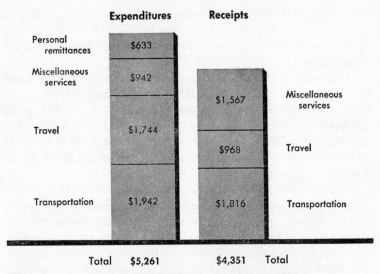

FIG. 15. Services and personal remittances in 1960 (in millions of dollars).
Source: Survey of Current Business.

marine is at a competitive disadvantage because of higher American wage levels. The gap between our income and expenses for transportation has been kept small only by substantial government subsidies to the United States merchant marine which permit it to set rates competitive with shipping lines under other flags and a regulation requiring that 50 percent of United States aid shipments be carried in United States ships. Still greater subsidies to swing more freight into United States ships do not seem sound economically, so there is little prospect of aiding our balance of payments situation in this area.

The travel account reflects primarily the much larger flow of American tourists to foreign lands as compared with that of other people coming to the United States. Once a luxury reserved for the upper classes, a vacation abroad is now practical for a great variety of Americans, from farmers to secretaries to small-town businessmen. In 1959, 705,000 Americans visited Europe and another 677,000 journeyed to the Caribbean and Latin America. The number who went to Canada and Mexico is not known, but thousands of Americans undoubtedly piled into the family car and headed north or south across our borders. It is safe to guess that close to 2 million Americans took their vacations in a foreign country in 1961. They all spent money — a total of $2.4 billion in 1959 — part of it showing up in the transportation account and the rest composing most of the travel account.

By contrast, the flow of foreign tourists into the United States has been modest. In 1959, 233,000 Europeans and 243,000 people from the Caribbean and Latin America visited us. Adding in the unknown influx from Mexico and Canada, the total was probably well below 1 million. The resultant income from travel of less than $1.0 billion leaves a wide gap which is an appreciable factor in our balance of payments deficit.

There is some hope that this gap can be narrowed at least a little. The massive flow of American tourists abroad is due in part to the aggressive promotion campaigns of foreign tourist bureaus. Americans have been bombarded with advertising, publicity stories, and other promotion devices playing up the joys of a foreign vacation. The Sunday supplements are jammed with ads selling Norwegian cruises, tours of the Alps, relaxation in the warmth of Acapulco, and the like.

By contrast, the United States has done little to attract foreigners here. Airlines, tour agencies, and other individual enterprises have done some promotion. But the total effort has been piddling compared with the programs of other countries. Now, however, our government is making a concentrated effort to make up for lost time. With $2.5 million appropriated by Congress in 1961, the Department of Commerce has launched a program of tourist advertising and promotion abroad like that which other countries have used here. This investment could well add $100 to $200 million to our tourism earnings, a small but constructive and useful increment to ease the balance of payments problem.

A modest contribution to the payments problem was also made by the reduction in September, 1961, in the amount of goods each American tourist may bring home duty-free from $500 to $100. The idea of the change is to decrease the amount that American tourists spend abroad. How much effect it will have is hard to estimate. Most tourists, even under the old law, brought in less than $100 worth of goods. Many may still bring in more than that despite the duty. The lady who enjoys picking out silk scarves and other Italian specialities in Roman shops as presents for an assortment of relatives and friends may not be deterred by the tariff on her excess imports.

The man who gets a good buy on an expensive Swiss watch or a German camera abroad may still come out ahead even after he pays the duty. Because of these uncertainties the estimates of the gains from the change range from a high of $150 million, figured by Treasury officials, to half or a quarter of that amount estimated by other experts.

The miscellaneous category covers a variety of services. One of the large items is communications, a field in which American companies have a dominant position. A large portion of international cable and radio messages are handled by International Telephone & Telegraph Company and similar American concerns. Other items included are film rentals and postal services. All told, our income from these services has consistently run ahead of expenditures, the net gain being $600 million in 1960. We probably will continue with this advantage, but the nature of the services involved is such that only minor changes can be expected; hence they are not a factor one way or the other in the current balance of payments problem.

Private remissions are a different type of item. They are composed of the myriads of small payments which Americans send to relatives in their home lands, a tradition which started many years ago when the massive tide of immigrants came here at the turn of the century. Thousands of Americans feel strong ties with their relatives across the sea, and a sense of obligation to share with them the good fortune they have found in the land of opportunity. The amount of the remissions has grown slowly but steadily over the years, standing now at about $600 million per year. It is a clear net loss in the balance of payments but it is unthinkable that it should be checked. It is probably best to look on it as a small but steady flow of private foreign aid contributing materially and spiritually to the bonds which hold the free world together.

Government Programs

The group of items shown in Figure 16 composing the government account is the major negative factor in our balance of payments. They include the contributions and loans made under various technical, economic, and military aid programs as well as the support of our military forces abroad. Because of its large negative impact, the government account has been singled out by many people as the source of our balance of payments problem. However, it does not appear to be a major factor in the sudden deficits of the past three years. The total amount in the government account has fluctuated between $4.3 billion and $6.2 billion for over ten years and the current level, although on the high side of this range, is, for example, just $500 million above 1956.

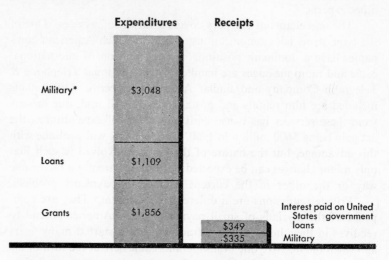

*Excluding exports of military goods (see text).
FIG. 16.   Government account for 1960 (in millions of dollars).
Source: Survey of Current Business.

Furthermore, the chief changes have been in the loans, which tend to be offset by comparable changes in exports. Most of them are used to finance purchase of American products. About half of the new loans in recent years have been by the Export-Import Bank, which finances only American exports. In 1961, the bank made loans to the Philippines for a steel plant, to Chile for railway improvements, and so on. In each case the money was used to buy American products, steel mill equipment for the Philippine project, locomotives for the Chilean railways, and so on; hence the loans result in comparable increases in exports. Another 25 percent of the loans are under Public Law 480, which finances the export of American agricultural surpluses. For example, we lend India $100,000 under PL 480, but the Indians must use the money to buy wheat from the United States; hence our exports rise by an equal amount. The remaining loans are made by the Development Loan Fund and other agencies. A large portion of these are also tied to purchase of American products. There has been considerable controversy over whether this "tied aid" is a sound practice. It means in some instances that the foreign recipients get less benefit per dollar than they would by buying less expensive equipment from Europe, Japan, or other sources. But it is in fact generally accepted at the moment, so very little of the loan money is spent outside the United States.

Of the grant money, a large portion is spent for the maintenance of American technical aid personnel abroad, much is used to buy supplies in the recipient countries, and some $500 million is estimated to be used for purchasing products in other countries.[1] Thus only a small portion of this is tied to American exports. But the grant totals over the past ten years have been very stable, ranging between $2.1 and $1.8 billion since 1952; hence one cannot single them out as a cause of the recent balance of payments deficits.

The military expenditures, although fluctuating considerably, do show a steady upward trend, rising from $1.3 billion in 1951 to a peak of $3.4 billion in 1958 and falling slightly to $3.0 billion in 1960. There were also $1,765 million of exports of military goods in 1960 but these are not included in either the exports (Figure 14) or the government account because they are equal and offset each other. An army tank shipped abroad is actually an export and an item of government overseas expenditure. But since no cash is exchanged it is customary to exclude it from the export totals as well as from the military expenses. Thus the full $3,048 millions shown were spent for local procurement abroad and maintenance of our armed forces in foreign bases. Of the 1960 total, about half was spent in Europe and smaller amounts were spent in Japan and other countries. There is a small offsetting income from the sale of military surplus goods abroad amounting to $335 million in 1960.

Our aid and military budgets involve questions of foreign policy and national security which by themselves could be the subject of another book. I can therefore consider them here only from the point of view of their balance of payments effects. Because virtually all the loans and a portion of the grants come right back to the United States in payment for exports, net contributions to our payments deficits can come only from cuts in the portions of these items spent abroad.

There is some room for change in the military account. Much of the current overseas procurement was undertaken in the early

1950's, when there was a general dollar shortage abroad and we were trying to help other countries to earn more so they could pay for American exports and be less dependent on American aid. Overseas procurement officers were instructed to give preference to local suppliers over domestic American sources. We therefore started to buy a great variety of products abroad which had been procured in the United States: flashlight batteries from Japanese manufacturers, truck parts from German firms, and so on. The dollar shortage, at least for Europe, of course disappeared some time ago, but the government, with characteristic administrative inertia, continued its local procurement policies. In October, 1960, however, the military finally caught up with the times, and a new order was issued calling for procurement of goods in the United States unless costs from foreign sources were lower. In addition, our government is trying to persuade European governments to shoulder more of the joint defense burden. An important gain in this direction was achieved in late 1961 with the assumption by the Germans of military costs in their country, saving the United States about $300 million per year.

In the economic aid area a large portion of the overseas expenditures which do not finance American exports are for the maintenance of technicians and others working in foreign countries. A considerable portion of the sums are paid to United States aid personnel who return much of their income to the United States; hence there is no net balance of payments loss. Reduction of the portion of these expenses which does stay abroad would amount to a cutback in our foreign aid program, which, as I have indicated, is a subject beyond the scope of this book. The balance of the overseas outlays is for procurement of goods either locally or from other countries. Reducing the local procurement in underdeveloped countries is so illogical in the context of the aid program that it cannot be considered. It certainly would make no sense to ship products all the way from the United States to India under the guise of foreign aid when the same products could be purchased in India.

But the roughly $500 million of United States aid which has been spent in buying goods from other sources, say Japan or Germany, for shipment to underdeveloped countries does offer some opportunity for change. Currently the sources for procurement are determined on the basis of cost, permitting the aid recipients to get the most value out of the aid budget. For example, we may contribute $100,000 for a technical center in Nigeria. The scientific equipment required might cost $40,000 if bought in the United States and only $34,000 from Germany or Japan. As Nigeria, like every underdeveloped country, has more needs for money than it can fill, such a saving will be applied directly to other productive projects. Thus requiring that grant money be spent in the United States would reduce the effectiveness of our aid.

But there is an alternative which is more promising: to persuade the other exporting countries to assume a greater share of the aid program. Our government has been working toward this end for some time and with at least moderate success. The most conspicuous evidence was the formation in December, 1960, of the Organization for Economic Cooperation and Development (OECD) including the European nations, Canada, and the United States. The OECD is only a consultative agency and involves no commitments by the members. However, its formation indicates the serious intentions of the member nations. One of the objectives of OECD is to contribute to economic development through the flow of capital and technical assistance to the less-developed nations. Most of the member countries already have economic aid programs, and it is reasonable to hope that they will expand these, especially where the funds will be spent in buying their own exports. Thus we may hope either that the $500 million figure may be cut or that it will be channeled into projects for which procurement from the United States is economically justified so that it is offset by an increase in exports.

Long-term Investment Account

Figure 17 shows the long-term private investment account. The account includes both direct investments by private business in factories, mines, and other operations and portfolio investments — purchases of stocks and bonds by individuals, banks, and other investors.

The inflow of capital includes some direct investments for ventures in the United States by British, French, German, and other foreign companies. For example, when the British Bowater Paper Company built a plant in Tennessee and Olivetti bought a part interest in Underwood, their investments showed up in this item. There is also an inflow of foreign money buying this country's stocks and bonds on Wall Street. But the total flow of long-term private investment into the United States is quite small, adding up to only $297 million in 1960.

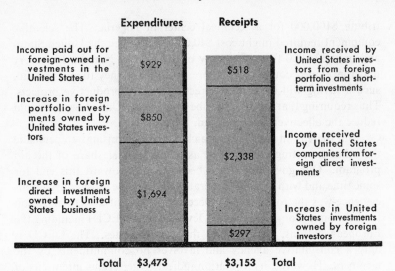

FIG. 17.   Long-term private investment account for 1960 (in millions of dollars).

By contrast, the outflow of American capital has been large. Looking back over the past few years it is apparent that it has been a major factor in our balance of payments deficits. From 1951 through 1955 new direct investments averaged $700 million per year. Then suddenly the figure jumped to $1,859 million in 1956 and has continued at that general level ever since.

Behind this surge of new investments lies the evolution of our overseas business, related in Chapter 1, especially as applied to the European boom. American companies have rushed to maintain their position in the European market, first as the boom got under way and then as the Common Market took shape. They reasoned, probably quite correctly, that if they did not jump quickly they might lose out on the tremendous opportunities which were developing. European companies and American competitors were moving fast, and quick action was needed to grab and hold a share of the market. As a result new European investments have been made in the past few years by hundreds of companies, ranging from the giants like Ford and General Motors to smaller companies like Rust-Oleum, of whom the average American has never heard (it makes protective paints).

Not all this increase in direct investment is a net loss to our balance of payments. According to a study by *Business Week* mentioned in Chapter 1, about 40 percent of the direct investments are used to purchase American machinery for overseas factories and thus are offset by a rise in our exports. The remaining 60 percent, however, is spent abroad. In a typical case, a company manufacturing electrical equipment will invest $1,000,000 in a new plant in France. To equip the plant it will send $400,000 of specialized machinery over from the United States. The remaining $600,000 will be spent to build the plant, obtain some simpler pieces of machinery from local suppliers, and pay for materials, labor, and other costs in the first months while the new factory is getting into operation. All these local expenditures are a direct drain on our balance of payments. Figuring that the annual rate of new direct investments has jumped around $1 billion in the past few years, we can estimate that 60 percent of that or around $600 million has been spent locally.

The remainder of the long-term investments — the purchases of foreign stocks and bonds by American investors — added up to $850 million in 1960. This also is a rise from the early 1950's, when Americans were buying foreign securities at a rate of about $300 million per year. Again the cause is to be found in the European boom. The rapid expansion of industries abroad has caught the fancy of Wall Street in the past few years, and American investors have been eagerly buying the stocks of European firms. There is no compensating increase in exports from this sort of investment; hence any increase in the rate of portfolio investments is all added to the balance of payments deficit. In all, then, we have about $500 million drain from portfolio investments and $600 million from direct investments or something around $1.1 billion of the change in our balance of payments since the early 1950's accounted for by the long-term investments.

Largely offsetting this factor, however, have been the earnings of the investments, especially those from direct investments. The inflow from the latter has risen from $1.3 billion in 1950 to $2.3 billion in 1960. We must take into consideration that the payments of earnings to foreigners for their investments have also increased by some $400 million in the same period. But this still leaves a net gain in earnings from American investments of around $600 million. Deducting this from the $1.1 billion drain from the new investments, we can account for around $500 million of the increase in the balance of payments deficit in recent years by changes in the long-term investment account.

The sharp rise in the outflow of long-term capital in the past few years has led many people to label it as the major villain in the payments problem, and a variety of proposals to restrain new direct investments have been advanced. Senator Gore raised the capital outflow issue as a supplement to his "exporting jobs" thesis to doubly damn American overseas investment (Chapter 1). Secretary Dillon used this as a prime argument in his testimony supporting the taxation of retained overseas profits (Chapter 4).

In considering the wisdom of reducing the investment flow we can take up where we left off in Chapter 1. Two main points emerged from that analysis: (1) that direct investments usually resulted from government restrictions or competitive pressures as the only way to maintain a position in foreign markets, and (2) that they retained some portion of the exports they displaced through purchase of American equipment and supplies. Although these points would imply that reducing the outflow of capital would be adverse to exports, a moderate reduction would probably not do much immediate harm. The key question is how managements would respond.

A survey of companies accounting for 40 percent of our foreign manufacturing made in 1961 by *The International Executive* revealed that a reduction in American funds available abroad would not result in a comparable reduction in their foreign factory expansion plans.[2] The companies would make up some 30 percent of the difference by obtaining local funds (e.g., bank loans) and there would be greater use of licensing and joint ventures, arrangements in which the need for American capital is minimized. The critical point in management thinking is the absolute necessity of going ahead with manufacturing plans lest markets be completely lost.

As previously noted, about 40 percent of the capital outflow is used to purchase American machinery. If the outflow were reduced moderately, it seems most likely that these expenditures would continue and the full reduction would be taken out of the money expended overseas. The electrical equipment manufacturer mentioned earlier provides a good example. If he abandoned his plans for a new plant in France, he would risk losing a foothold in the whole European market. So, if the government restricted the outflow of American capital, he would work out the best alternative he could to be sure that the production plans kept rolling. As likely as not, the solution would be to find in France most of the $600,000 used for local expenses. He might sell some bonds or stocks to French investors to raise $300,000 with which to build the plant and borrow another $300,000 from French banks to cover the cost of the labor, supplies, and so on, needed to get the plant in operation. Presumably some export of American capital would still be possible, and this would permit sending over the $400,000 of specialized machinery from the United States. Other companies would react in different ways, but on the whole we can assume that the immediate effect of a moderate reduction of capital outflow (say of 25 percent, or about $500 million) would be a direct improvement in our balance of payments with no apparent loss to our position in overseas markets or our exports.

But to decide on this basis that we should cut back on our direct investments is to take a very short-range view of the situation. What is lacking is a full appreciation of the impact of long-term investments on our balance of payments as a source of continuing future earnings. It is possible to cite instances in which the outflow of capital has exceeded the return of earnings. For example, in his testimony Secretary Dillon pointed out that, in the period 1957–1960, $1.7 billion of new capital flowed into Western Europe while only $1.3 billion of dividends returned.[3] But this is a case in which investments have been increasing very rapidly, distorting the normal relationships.

It is more informative to look at the total flow and its trend over the years. In the total balance of payments for 1960 our income from private investments exceeded the outflow of capital by $400 million ($2.9 billion vs. $2.5 billion). In the decade from 1951 through 1960 the net return was an even more impressive $9.1 billion ($21.3 billion vs. $12.2 billion). Thus on a long-term basis our investments have been a very substantial contributor on the positive side of our balance of payments.

The issue then really boils down to whether a short-run gain from reducing investments is now in the national interest. Because the earnings come from old rather than new investments, a reduction in capital outflow would not cut the return flow of profits and we would thus for the moment have the benefit of our past investments without the current dollar drain. We would not feel the loss from the reduced rate of investment for several years because the typical new investment does not start to pay out dividends for several years. Most companies provide a small amount of capital for a new operation and then expect to finance growth out of retained earnings. It is not until it has achieved considerable maturity that an operation has enough extra cash to start paying dividends back to the parent.

By sound financial standards, however, this seems very poor reasoning upon which to cut back the flow of investment. We can quite realistically liken the position of the United States to that of an individual. It is considered sound practice for individuals to save some of their money and invest it in ways which will produce greater income in the future. This is what our overseas investments are doing for us. Currently their earnings are running about 11 percent of the investments, 8 percent being sent home to the United States and the remaining 3 percent being reinvested to bring us yet greater earnings in the future.

On this basis most people would commend foreign investment in normal times as a form of national thrift. Now the question arises whether, under the present abnormal deficit payments conditions, a reduction of investment is sound. When an individual runs into financial trouble we consider it quite acceptable for him to stop saving and even draw upon past savings. Is the United States in a comparable situation? The answer is a matter of judgment. Some very competent people feel that the potential financial crisis is so threatening that we must act, and they feel that the sacrifice of some future earnings by cutting investments is one of the least costly steps we can take.

On the other hand, there are those who feel that while corrective steps in other aspects of our international transactions are harder, they are fundamentally sounder and that this is a very inopportune moment to be restricting investments. With the European economy expanding rapidly and industry in a formative stage in the developing economies, we are passing through a period of prime international investment opportunities, in sharp contrast, for example, to the sluggish thirties. This is a time when, visualizing ourselves as a single national investor, we would be very wise to pull our belt in a notch or two and throw all the resources we can into investments which promise to bring a very handsome return in the future.

In addition, a second look at the question of exports and business opportunities is in order. I indicated above that a moderate reduction in investments would probably not reduce plans for manufacturing expansion abroad but would, rather, reorient these companies to greater use of licensees and joint ventures. So long as the manufacturing ventures remain under United States control, we may expect to retain the income from the 10 percent or so of their supplies that, as we noted in Chapter 1, they purchase from the United States.

But as the operations shift toward joint ventures and licensing arrangements in which a large portion or all of the investment funds come from local sources so that control rests in foreign hands, the chance of losing export volume increases.

An American management will always give a preference when it can to purchases from the parent company because that adds to its ultimate profits. But a foreign management is less likely to favor American products because it has stronger ties with local suppliers, it is more responsive to pressure from the national government for local procurement, and it has less to gain by buying from the United States. Thus we must add to the long-run loss of earnings from reduced investments a probable reduction in export income.

These arguments do not preclude reducing investments if the balance of payments deficit cannot be remedied by other means. But they do place it well down the list in order of desirable measures.

"Hot Money"

The items shown in Figure 18 cover short-term capital movements and gold transfers as well as some unaccounted for transactions. Short-term capital is money put into bank accounts or

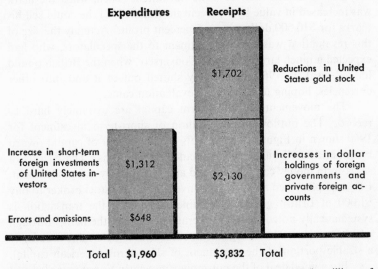

Expenditures	Receipts
	$1,702 — Reductions in United States gold stock
Increase in short-term foreign investments of United States investors — $1,312	$2,130 — Increases in dollar holdings of foreign governments and private foreign accounts
Errors and omissions — $648	
Total $1,960	$3,832 Total

FIG. 18. Short-term capital, dollar holdings and gold for 1960 (in millions of dollars).

invested in securities maturing in less than a year. Most of it is used to purchase government bills and notes with maturities of ninety days, six months, or a year.

This type of capital moves between countries to avoid risks of war, political trouble, and the like, and for two profit-oriented reasons: (1) to take advantage of high interest rates, and (2) to profit from exchange rate changes. Short-term interest rates vary considerably from time to time. In the United States the rates on Treasury bills ranged from 0.5 percent to 4.5 percent between 1958 and 1960; those of other countries show similar variations. "Hot money," as short-term capital is often called, is quick to shift toward countries with high rates.

Profiting from exchange rate changes is a form of speculation. The trick is to have your money in a currency which increases in value and not in one which decreases in value. For example, the German balance of payments position was so strong during 1960 that many people expected that the value of the mark would be increased. The typical American exchange speculator bought, let us say, $10,000 worth of German currency — 42,000 marks at the 1960 exchange rate. He may have invested the marks in German securities or, as likely as not, merely put them into a German bank account, where they earned a little interest while he waited. Then, when the mark was increased in value by 5 percent in March, 1961, he could sell his marks for $10,500 dollars, or a 5 percent profit. Actually the size of this revaluation was a disappointment to the speculators, who had expected a much larger change. Conversely, when the British pound looked weak in 1961, hot money shifted out of it and into other currencies, hoping to profit if a devaluation came.

The movements of short-term capital are extremely hard to record. The outflow of $1.3 billion of short-term investment for 1960 shown in Figure 18 represents the movement of capital owned by Americans through regular financial institutions. These shifts of short-term money can be observed and recorded by our government. For example, when an American investor tells his stockbroker to buy $1,000 of British government, ninety-day bills, the transaction is systematically noted by the brokerage house and the banks through which it works. Thus the government is able to determine accurately a sizable portion of the movement of short-term American capital.

But a good deal of the hot-money movement is not recorded and shows up in the "errors and omissions" figure. To understand this situation we need to have a picture of the whole problem of gathering balance of payments data. Since our government does not have exchange controls, there is no single record of our foreign transactions. The data must therefore be assembled from a variety of sources — export declarations, customs reports for imports, bank reports of foreign accounts, and the like. Each of the items we have discussed so far is the result of careful statistical checks on transactions which can be openly observed in some phase of our international dealings. But this system is not complete, and the difference between the computed items is recorded as "errors and omissions."

It is generally assumed that this figure is largely short-term capital because of the nature of these financial dealings. The international transactions which are hardest to check are the dealings of the "smart money crowd," who shift their funds from country to country to take advantage of exchange rate and interest rate fluctuations. Much of this hot money moves in channels which, while not necessarily illegal, are difficult for government officials to observe. There are probably other gaps in the statistical system. Private remittances may be understated because people may slip a few dollar bills in a letter to Europe; similar inaccuracies doubtless misstate the tourism figure. But the magnitudes of these errors are small by comparison with the shifts of hot money; hence it is considered to be the chief component of the "errors and omissions" at least in 1960, when it recorded a large outflow of dollars paralleling that of short-term capital.

The third item, the foreign dollar holdings, is composed of foreign accounts in American banks, short-term dollar investments held by foreigners, and their holdings of long-term United States government bonds.

These changes in foreign dollar holdings are commonly grouped with gold movements to indicate that they are the items by means of which the United States settles its international accounts. International transactions are by definition balancing. Each involves offsetting entries somewhere in the balance of payments such as those shown in Figure 19: each dollar of exports is matched by an equal drop in foreign dollar holdings or increase in our gold stock, each increase in American investments is offset by a decrease in our dollar position (an increase in foreign dollar holdings) and so on. The transactions we have already discussed are the primary international exchanges of business, finance, and so on. Dollar holdings and gold are dependent upon them, their net change being the means for covering any payments deficit or being paid off for any surplus.

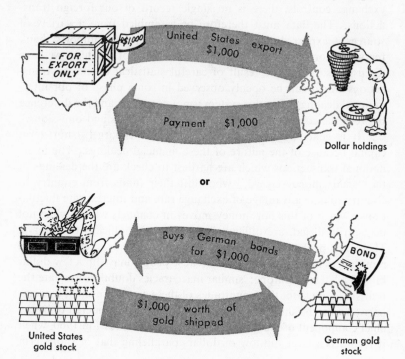

FIG. 19.   The balanced flow of international transactions.

There is one complication in this otherwise neat picture. The foreign dollar holdings are of two types. Some of them are funds maintained in the United States as foreign government reserves or by businesses to use for commercial purposes. The remainder is short-term capital placed in the United States for investment purposes. Changes in the first category are true balancing items in the international accounts, for they are specifically intended for use in financing international transactions. Changes in the second category are really primary items and they should properly be recorded separately in the same way as the changes in short-term investments owned by Americans.

Unfortunately it is not possible to separate the two types because both take the same physical form (investment in United States government notes, for example). Thus in thinking about the short-term capital item of $1.3 billion shown in Figure 18 we must bear in mind that it gives only one side of the picture — the movement of the American-owned portion of international hot money. Since foreign-owned hot money probably moves in the same direction as American-owned hot money, it is a safe assumption that addition of the former would always magnify the fluctuations of the latter, whether they be inflow or outflow.

Returning, then, to the short-term capital item of $1.3 billion, we can consider it to reflect only part of the shift of funds by short-term investors. The direction of its change is probably a true indication of the change in the total, but the magnitude of the changes may be double or more that shown. All this is important because the short-term item has become an important factor in our deficit. Through most of the postwar period, the short-term capital movements were relatively small. There was a fairly steady outflow due to the generally higher interest rates abroad, but the changes were minor in the total payments situation. From 1950 to 1959 it averaged $210 million per year. The highest figure was $600 million in 1954; in 1959 only $100 million went abroad.

In 1960, however, there was a sudden sharp rise of about $1 billion in the outflow, which, combined with the "errors and omissions" change and a probably parallel movement in the foreign holdings, suggests that as much as $2 billion of short-term capital left the United States. Behind this is a two-year history of rapid changes in world money market conditions. In 1959, United States short-term interest rates rose sharply, government bills hitting 4.5 percent and thus attracting investors, as indicated by a decline in the outflow of American short-term money to $100 million. During 1960, the United States government bill rates fell sharply to the 2.5 percent range. At the same time European governments, especially in Germany and Britain, were holding their interest rates in the 5 to 6 percent range to dampen down their booms and threatened inflation. Smart money therefore quickly shifted its attention to Europe, causing a massive outflow that was certainly the biggest single factor in the deficit for that year.

The movements of hot money in and out of the United States are not a fundamental cause of our payments difficulties, and reducing them will not, therefore, correct any long-term imbalance. But the magnitude and suddenness of the shifts, especially in 1959 and 1960 did considerably aggravate the situation, and similar experiences should be avoided if possible.

Direct restrictions would serve this purpose, but they are not really desirable, partly because we are trying to reduce rather than increase controls and partly because, despite its speculative character, short-term capital often serves a useful function. For example, the rise in interest rates in the United States in late 1959 was caused in part by the inventory build-up before the steel strike, for which considerable short-term capital was required. An influx of European money helped meet this demand.

It is more constructive, therefore, to attack the problem at its roots by removing the incentives for sudden shifts of hot money, notably major interest rate changes and currency crises.

Dealing with short-term interest rates is greatly complicated by government fiscal policies designed to regulate domestic economies. One of the standard techniques for restraining a boom is to force interest rates up, thereby discouraging installment sales, inventory buying, and so on. Likewise, interest rates are lowered to encourage the same activities. Until 1960 the United States government used these techniques freely without regard to the balance of payments; the Treasury bill rate for example, as noted above, was reduced almost to 0.5 percent during the 1958 recession and raised to 4.5 percent in the boom late in 1959. But in the 1960–1961 recession the government was forced to think twice about the balance of payments effect and allowed the rate to fall only to around 2.5 percent. On the other side of the ocean, during 1960, both Germany and England lowered their bank rates, which control the short-term interest rates, to reduce the differential between their rates and those in the United States and thus minimize the movement of short-term money. Domestic fiscal policy considerations are usually far more important than the balance of payments impact. However, these recent government actions indicate that within limits it is possible to temper interest rate changes to reduce the flow of short-term capital.

Currency crises are significant because short-term capital will tend to move out of currencies which seem weak and likely to be devalued into those which are strong. In doing so, such a movement of course still further weakens the precarious currency and may hasten the devaluation. Thus measures which minimize the possibilities of exchange rate changes will also reduce the flow of hot money. A prime cause of postwar devaluations has been inflation. France,

Brazil, and other countries which have had severe inflation have seen their exchange rates fall sharply. One of the important reasons for fighting inflation in the United States is to avoid this risk. A substantial rise of our internal prices could so aggravate the export lag problem that a devaluation might be forced upon us. But in the present state of affairs there is, as we have noted, little chance that the United States dollar would be devalued. We are more concerned, therefore, with the problem of currency crises concerning other countries and the resulting shifts of hot money around the world. Dealing with this problem brings us into the much broader question of international reserves, which requires separate discussion in the next chapter.

A Light Hand on the Balance

From this analysis it is quite clear why there is so much disagreement and debate over the state of our balance of payments. It is evident that its major components are capable of large and independent movements. It is probably more "normal," therefore, to have substantial gaps than a balancing of their net effect. There is certainly no over-all problem upon which one can fix attention. Much of the recent difficulty seems to arise from large changes of a transitory nature — the fluctuations in exports of raw and semi-processed materials, the surge of direct investment in Europe, and the sudden shift of short-term capital to Europe. The only adverse factor which seems to have a sustained trend is the military expenditures item, but its rise has not been great. The significant increases in government loans are largely offset by increases in exports.

Some people have concluded from all this that the deficits of the last three years are due to an unusual combination of circumstances and that there is no basic problem. Indeed, they reason that a reversal of fortune might just as well result in a surplus in a year or two. But this school of thought has been losing ground as the large deficits have continued, and most people now feel that positive action is required to strengthen our position.

There are, as we have seen, a variety of possibilities, and in each we must consider other, and often more important, effects beyond the balance of payments. Furthermore, the points at which actions should be taken are not necessarily those which have caused the present deficits. The complex of our international transactions is a dynamic, evolving set of activities in which the past is by no means a standard for the future. Thus we cannot look only to the elements which have caused the recent imbalances. Rather, we must approach each item with an open mind, considering whether or not we can and should attempt to alter its size and giving more weight to its future implications than to any past record. Viewing the situation in this perspective we can see that there are several points at which corrective action seems both feasible and constructive: stimulating exports and tourism in the United States, reducing overseas military procurement, and persuading other nations to assume more of the foreign-aid load. Only when the full possibilities of these measures have been exhausted should we consider the negative moves which do not seem in our best long-run interests — restricting imports and reducing long-term capital investment.

■■■■■■■■■■■ 6

On the Brink
of Bankruptcy

Is the United States close to bankruptcy in its international finances?
Shocking as it seems this is a highly pertinent question for us to ask. We are unlikely, at least at the present, really to go bankrupt, and we do have resources to fall back on. Yet the cold mathematics of our international accounts shown in Figure 20 portrays a picture of a precarious financial position: we could not today lay our hands readily on enough hard money to meet the current claims against us.

By the end of 1960 foreign governments, businesses, and individuals had built up bank deposits and holdings of short-term investments in the United States of $17.4 billion. To this must be added their $1.4 billion worth of longer-term United States government bonds which they regard as liquid assets and the $4.7 billion of current claims which international institutions, notably the International Monetary Fund, can make on us. In all, the liquid claims against United States currency added up to $23.5 billion.

To meet these claims our chief asset is our gold stock, which stood at $17.8 billion at that time. But $12 billion of the gold is not available because it must be held by the Federal Reserve Banks as a 25 percent reserve against their total note and deposit liabilities. There was a proposal by the Kennedy administration in 1961 to eliminate the reserve requirement and make the full gold stock available. However, it was not acted upon by Congress and it is questionable because it removes an important pressure for responsible fiscal policy. So there was only $5.8 billion of really liquid assets to meet the $23.5 billion of potential demands. In addition, of our $4.1

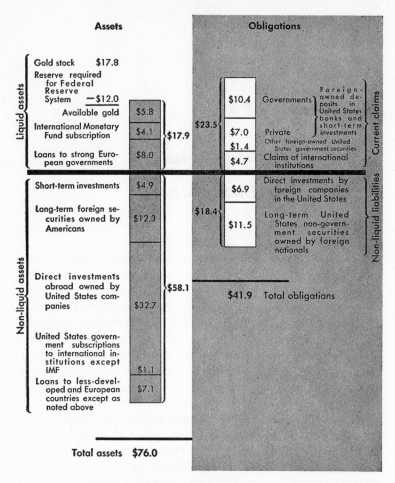

FIG 20. International assets and obligations of the United States, December 31, 1960 (in billions of dollars).
Sources: The International Position of the Dollar, Committee for Economic Development, and *Survey of Current Business.*

billion subscription to the International Monetary Fund, one quarter can be readily withdrawn, and the balance may also be considered semiliquid. Likewise, $8 billion of loans to various financially strong European governments are relatively available. These were made to the British, Germans, and others in the postwar period. Although the repayments are formally scheduled for future dates, they may be paid off sooner to help us in a financial crisis. In fact, the Germans made a $587 million prepayment of a loan in 1961 to ease our situation. But that still gives only $17.9 billion to offset the $23.5 billion of obligations.

Our total assets exceed our liabilities by a large amount. As Figure 20 shows, all our international assets at the end of 1960 added up to $76 billion against total obligations of $41.9 billion. But our other assets are not readily available to meet current foreign obligations against us: $4.9 billion of foreign short-term securities held by Americans, $12.3 billion of foreign stocks and bonds owned by American private investors, $32.7 billion of direct investments of American companies in overseas operations which could not be liquidated without major loss, $1.1 billion of United States government subscriptions to the World Bank and other international institutions which are permanent obligations, and $7.1 billion of loans to weaker European countries and underdeveloped nations which are in no position to make advance payments. The government might require American investors to liquidate their short- and long-term investments, but that would be such a serious step that it would surely precipitate a financial crisis which would be as bad as bankruptcy.

Piling Up the Debt

Our present financial predicament is the result of our balance of payments deficits and the special position of the United States dollar as an international currency. As we saw in the previous chapter, the United States paid out $12.6 billion more over the period 1958–1961 in its international dealings than it received. For most countries, such large and sustained deficits would have caused a financial crisis long ago. Because they have to settle their international accounts with gold or dollars, they cannot run up deficits much beyond their reserves. France, for example, held at the end of 1961 about $1.6 billion in gold and about $1.2 billion of dollar accounts in United States banks or other short-term international assets. If the French have a balance of payments deficit they must pay for it out of these reserves. The nation might borrow to strengthen its reserves, but this is a temporary expedient and the day of reckoning must come.

But the United States operates on a different basis because of the use of the dollar as an international currency. The manner in which our deficits have been financed is shown in Figure 21. We have paid for a large portion of our needs with gold — $1.7 billion in 1960, for example. The mass of gold we have been piling up in Fort Knox is so great that this loss has not weakened our financial status in itself. It is the method of financing the other portion of our deficit which is peculiar and which makes the decline in our gold reserves dangerous.

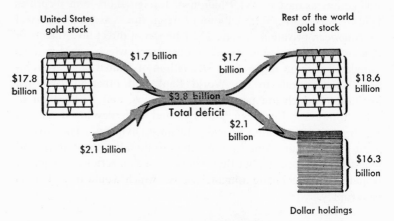

FIG. 21.   Financing the 1960 United States balance of payments deficit.

In 1960, $2.1 billion of deficits was settled by adding to the bank accounts and other liquid dollar holdings of foreigners. There are a variety of technical aspects to this but the system amounts, in effect, to paying for the deficit with IOU's. We can follow its workings in our dealings with a fictitious country, Padua, in 1961. Our exporters sold $4 million of goods to businessmen in Padua and we imported $4.5 million from Padua. All this was financed through the Bank of Padua, which had an account of $1 million in the XYZ Bank in New York at the start of 1961.

When a Paduan exporter sold, say, $1,000 worth of textiles to the United States, he received a dollar draft as payment and gave it to the Bank of Padua for collection (Figure 22). The bank paid the exporter the equivalent of $1,000 in Paduan currency. It then sent the draft to the XYZ Bank, which collected the $1,000 from the American importer and credited this amount to the account of the Bank of Padua.

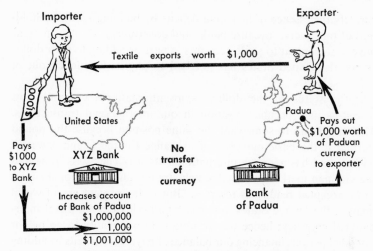

FIG. 22. How the United States imports without losing dollars or gold.

When an American exporter sold to Padua, the process was simply reversed. The American exporter accepted payment from the Paduan importer through the banking system. The importer paid Paduan currency into the Bank of Padua and the XYZ Bank paid off the American exporter out of the account of the Bank of Padua. In neither case did any money actually move between Padua and the United States.

At the end of the year the net effect of all these individual transactions was to increase the account of the Bank of Padua in the XYZ Bank by the amount of our deficit in trade with Padua — $500,000. The Bank of Padua could have drawn down this account by buying gold from the United States, but it had no particular use for gold. The bank account at least earned a little interest, and it was convenient to have it as a base from which to handle transactions not only in American-Paduan trade but in Paduan trade with other countries as well. All over the world, banks, businessmen, and governments accepted drafts for dollars in the XYZ Bank as sound currency; hence a large dollar account was a valuable asset for Padua's international dealings.

This example is considerably simplified. Our main deficits have, of course, been due more to complex investment and government dealings than to trade imbalance. And there is a good deal of rigmarole to the banking operations. But the story describes ac-

curately the essence of financing deficits by building up dollar holdings of foreigners. Because banks and governments of other nations
have been content to settle accounts in part by adding to their dollar
assets, the United States has not had to pay its full deficit out of
gold reserves.

The status of the dollar as an international currency thus
places us in a peculiar position in our international transactions.
The British are in somewhat the same position because the pound
sterling is the basic currency of exchange for the Commonwealth
nations and has a strong international status. The Swiss franc and
the German mark also have enough strength in international circles
to be accepted readily as reserves. But in the present era of world
finance, the United States dollar is by all odds the dominant international currency; hence we are unique in our ability to go on for
extended periods financing our balance of payments deficits by adding
to our current obligations to other nations.

A Childish Game

All this has been very convenient for both the United States and
its trading partners. But as Jacques Rueff, one of Europe's foremost
financial experts, observes, it is a dangerous process: "The country
with a key currency is in the deceptively euphoric position of never
having to pay off its international debts. The money it pays to foreign
creditors comes right back home, like a boomerang. . . The functioning of the international monetary system was thus reduced to a
childish game in which, after each round, the winners return their
marbles to the losers."[1]

From 1958 through 1961, the "childish game" permitted the
United States to incur an appallingly large balance of payments
deficit; it also resulted in increasing our liquid obligations to
foreigners by $6.1 billion. However convenient the game may have
been, our financial community now realizes that it cannot go on
forever. It is fundamentally unsound to continue such deficits,
and there must be a limit beyond which we cannot safely pile up
obligations in excess of our liquid assets. This realization has given
urgency to the various remedies for the balance of payments problem
discussed in the previous chapter. The ultimate solution for our
financial position lies in that direction. But, having got ourselves
into our current precarious financial predicament, we are forced to
take other measures to avert a possible financial crisis.

Avoiding a Run on the Bank

The chief hazard is the possibility of loss of confidence in the strength of the dollar. The whole structure now rests upon the willingness of the foreign claimants to leave their money in deposits and investments in the United States. This in turn depends upon their confidence that the United States dollar will retain its value and that the United States will be able to meet its obligations. If confidence in either of these points were to be lost, foreign governments and private claimants might be expected to demand payment in gold for their dollar holdings and we would have a first-class financial crisis. The risk of a "run" on the dollar of this sort is lessened by the power of foreign governments to restrict dollar withdrawals by their citizens and the strong interest of these governments in preserving the value of the dollar. But the risk is there and must be dealt with realistically.

In attacking this problem, financial experts have taken the adequacy of reserves as the key to confidence, and in doing so they have come up with solutions applicable not only to the United States problem but to the whole world. The American situation is peculiar, as we have seen, in that we can pile up balance of payments deficits by adding to foreign holdings. But when we come to the question of confidence, the essence of the problem is really no different from that of other countries. They will typically be forced to meet their payments deficits out of reserves immediately. We postpone the day of reckoning by adding to foreign dollar holdings, but ultimately those are demands against our gold and other liquid assets. So the strength of our currency as well as that of others rests, in the end, on reserves.

The objective of the financial experts has been, therefore, to reinforce the reserves of all countries to strengthen confidence in all currencies. Since confidence in the future value of currencies contributes greatly to encouraging long-term investments and trading among nations, this effort is a prime objective of our foreign economic policy.

The main thrust of the effort to stabilize currencies has been focused upon broadening the resources upon which a country can draw to supplement its reserves in an emergency. The International Monetary Fund (IMF), conceived in 1944, has been the chief mechanism for accomplishing that objective. The members, who comprise most of the nations of the free world, provide the resources of the

IMF according to a quota system. Each pays into the Fund in gold either 25 percent of its quota or 10 percent of its net official holdings of gold and United States dollars, whichever is smaller. The balance of the quota is paid in the member's own currency. The total resources of the IMF amount to about $14 billion.

Each member may draw on the IMF for gold or other currencies up to 200 percent of its quota when it needs to supplement its own reserves, and, in an emergency, the IMF is allowed to provide still further support. This system has helped a number of countries over difficult periods. For example, Britain borrowed $1.5 billion in 1961 to strengthen its reserves until it could achieve the basic corrections needed to bring its balance of payments into line. The United States has a right to draw up to $5.7 billion of gold or other currencies from the IMF.

But there is considerable feeling among international financial circles that this system is not adequate in size and flexibility. And there is some underlying concern at the extreme reliance upon the dollar as a reserve currency in view of the current United States deficits and the hazards of the "childish game" described by Jacques Rueff. The proposed remedies have ranged all the way from a simple expansion of the IMF to a plan advanced by Professor Robert Triffin of Yale University to convert the IMF into a world central bank. Under the Triffin plan each nation would turn over to the IMF a substantial portion of its present reserves. The IMF would then issue a form of currency which for discussion purposes are called X-dollars. The X-dollars would be used in the same way that United States dollars are used today as a medium of international exchange. Professor Triffin argues that this system would be beneficial in establishing a currency for international business which was independent of United States fiscal and balance of payments conditions and capable of direct expansion. The IMF would be able to issue more X-dollars as needed to meet the needs of the international financial community.

Critics of the plan are concerned, however, over its potential inflationary effect and the difficulties of assuring responsible control. It would clearly put considerable power to influence trading conditions and the situations of individual countries in the hands of a semiautonomous international agency.

Most government financial experts believe that the needs of the current international financial situation can be served adequately by expanding the resources of the International Monetary Fund. This was the consensus of the finance ministers and central bank officials of the member nations of the International Monetary Fund when they met in Vienna in the fall of 1961. They agreed on a plan which would permit the IMF to draw upon the major countries for funds in addition to the regular quotas as they were needed. A total of $6 billion of drawings would be possible: $2 billion from European nations, $1.0 billion from Britain, $1.0 billion from Canada, Sweden, and Japan and $2.0 billion from the United States.

Act Tough, Stay Calm

The psychological attitude of the United States toward our international financial position is a real enigma. The question with which this chapter opened is a matter of valid concern. We are financially in a precarious position. If our balance of payments deficits continue on the scale of the past few years a disastrous crisis could develop. However, the nations of the free world have a stake in the strength of the dollar and, because of their determination to shore it up, they have minimized the actual danger and will continue for some time to do so.

Thus the American public is shielded from the unpleasant financial facts. The rate of gold outflow has caused some public concern in recent years, but our ability to get by despite the losses has set people's minds at ease. And the efforts of other nations to provide additional reserves through the IMF have been reassuring. Thus there is no great sense of urgency among the public as, for example, there is over the unemployment situation.

This is at once good and bad. It would be most unfortunate if the public were in a state of panic over our financial condition. Nothing could be worse than a deterioration of confidence in the dollar accompanied by a great flight of short-term capital out of the dollar, with depressing effects on the domestic economy. We must certainly retain a sense of calm confidence in our ultimate ability to cope with the problem.

But calmness should not lead to complacency, for the problem is real and can become indeed serious. There is a clear need for action and in many cases for toughness. We must act with decisiveness to make the United States more competitive in export markets by restraining our inflation and pushing our economy to greater utilization of its capacity. We must bargain hard and firmly with our European allies on sharing the costs of helping the less-developed nations. We cannot retreat into protectionism, but to build our exports we must be firm in our insistence on tariff reductions abroad, especially by the European Common Market nations. In these and other ways we must work earnestly for a balancing of our international accounts so that our obligations to the rest of the world do not continue to mount higher above our current assets.

■■■■■■■■■■■■ **7**

Trading with
the Enemy

News item: "The Speed-Feed Company of Raleigh, Indiana, has announced the signing of a contract with the Russians for the sale of $40,000 worth of automatic machine tools. It is understood that the Russians will use the machinery incorporating Speed-Feed's patented high-speed tool-changing devices in manufacturing agricultural tractors."

Is this just another business transaction? Or is Speed-Feed in essence a traitor, playing into the hands of our enemies for a mess of pottage? Should we be doing business with the Russians at all? If so, how much? These are difficult but highly important questions. Americans still shudder at the memory of the scrap steel that we sold to the Japanese flying back in our faces from Pearl Harbor to Guadalcanal. No one wants to be part of a repetition of that disaster. Yet there are strong pressures to expand trade with the Russians. So we must look critically at East-West trade to determine just what is and what is not best for our national welfare.

Interest in doing business with the Russians has risen noticeably since the visit of Premier Khrushchev to the United States in 1959. He was clearly anxious to increase Russian imports from the United States to a level not seen since World War II. During the 1930's our exports to Russia had grown to a significant though not large total, running around $70 million per year. Throughout World War II we shipped large amounts of munitions and civilian goods to Russia under the Lend-Lease program. But after that, as the tempo of the Cold War increased, trading between the two countries fell sharply.

In 1952 it hit a low point, with American exports to Russia amounting to a mere $15,118. In the next few years shipments rose slowly, reaching $7,398,000 in 1959. Then came a tremendous jump to $38,368,000 in 1960.

Our trade with the Eastern European satellites of Russia has followed much the same pattern as that with Russia. The major exception is Poland. The 1956 uprisings which brought Wladyslaw Gomulka to power caused a major change in United States policy toward Poland. Our government decided there was some real hope that the Poles could maintain a degree of independence from Soviet domination. We therefore have extended substantial credits to Poland for the purchase of agricultural products, coal-mining machinery, and other nonstrategic goods, which we hoped would strengthen them in striving for greater independence. Under this stimulus, exports to Poland rose from a low point of $3,103,000 in 1955 to $143,091,000 in 1960. Communist China is not recognized by the United States and there is a complete embargo on trade with the Red Chinese. Our policies on trade with Poland and Red China arise from individual considerations which will not be explored here. But in broad terms both are dependent upon our policies toward Russia. We are well aware that, despite some degree of independence, the two countries are still under strong influence from Russia, and their economies are closely tied to Russia's.

Thus the central issue for the United States in the East-West trade is how to handle its relations with Russia. The policy question constantly before the United States government and our business community is the extent to which we should expand exports. Interwoven with that question are Russian policies on trade and aid with the rest of the world which indirectly affect our policies. To think through our course of action we must therefore have a picture of the whole Russian program for economic relations with the outside world.

What Are the Russians Up To?

To the Russians the ideal economy is autarky — complete self-sufficiency. They would prefer nothing better than to be entirely independent of the rest of the world, to live without any foreign trade at all. From a military point of view, this would provide maximum economic strength.

Russia has maintained a very high degree of autarky, with imports running around 1.2 percent of her Gross National Product compared with about 3.0 percent for the United States and much higher percentages in European countries. It is a costly policy, for it is in direct opposition to the principles of comparative advantage we discussed in Chapter 3. The Russians have not gone so far as growing bananas in greenhouses but they are making many things which could be imported less expensively. For example, while they import natural rubber, they are known to be making a considerable amount of synthetic rubber by relatively high-cost processes. But they would rather carry the higher costs so as to have the greater strategic independence.

But full autarky is not practical even for a nation reputed to have greater natural resources than the United States. Russia buys regularly from foreign sources a number of key commodities, such as coffee, which it cannot produce, and others, such as copper, which it produces in insufficient quantities. In all, raw materials, fuels, and food products make up about two-thirds of Russian imports. Presumably Russia could get along without some imports, such as cocoa, make do with ersatz coffee as the Germans did in World War II, and develop low-grade, higher-cost domestic sources for copper and other imported raw materials. But there apparently is a limit to her willingness to sacrifice some of the advantages of autarky to achieve more economical and satisfactory use of her resources.

Imports of raw materials from underdeveloped countries also serve a purpose in creating dependence upon Russia. For example, in 1960, 45 percent of Egypt's cotton exports were to the Soviet bloc, and, in all, the communist countries took about 50 percent of that country's exports. Such heavy dependence gives the Russians strong economic leverage to use for political ends.

The other third of Russian imports is composed of machinery and equipment, and it is these products which Khrushchev was looking for in the United States. The Russians have evidently reached a point where they are extremely anxious to obtain Western industrial know-how in the form of machinery and equipment to aid their economic expansion. This happened once before. In the early 1930's Russian industrial growth was hindered by lack of advanced technology. Stalin engineered a softening of relations with the West, culminating in formal recognition of his government by the Roosevelt administration in 1933. This opened the doors to greater trade, and the Russians imported a wide range of machinery, thus giving their industry a big boost.

Now the pressing needs seem to be primarily for chemical plants, though the Russians are looking for a wide range of other industrial gear. The impetus for the current drive was the Russian Seven Year Plan which started in 1958. The plan set high goals for expansion of the Russian economy, including quadrupling the production of chemicals. Western experts are generally agreed that the Russians cannot hope to achieve their targets by 1965 without drawing on the skills of the Western world. Khrushchev has said as much himself. In a speech in East Germany in July, 1958, he admitted Soviet inferiority in the production of chemicals and synthetics and proposed that it would be useful to import the experience and the advanced machinery of the West to "save time" in building up the Soviet industry. Then in a speech in Russia in February, 1959, he observed that "we are not ashamed to learn from the Germans" in overcoming industrial deficiencies.[1]

Besides the critical bottleneck in their chemical industry, the Russians are finding that as their industrial plant grows and diversifies it is full of gaps. They have achieved superiority in space rocketry but only by channeling into that one field of technology a great concentration of their limited scientific manpower. In 1000 and 1 other fields they still lag far behind the West, and as they strive for a major surge in economic production they have become acutely conscious of these gaps. One of the most important is the broad field of mechanized, semiautomated production. This is now a critical problem because the Russians are short of manpower. The wartime casualties and lag in births are showing up in a decline in new workers coming of age. Whereas there had been from 1 to 2 million new pairs of hands each year during the 1950's to accomplish production increases, the rate dropped below 1 million as the 1960's started.[2] Thus the Russians must get more output from each worker and that means more mechanization.

The extent of their interests in this direction was emphasized to me in 1959 while I was escorting a visiting team of four Russians, led by Dmitri Korolev, Deputy Minister of Trade of the Greater Russian Republic (the largest republic, which includes Moscow and Leningrad). The team was supposed to be interested in marketing, but it soon became apparent that their main preoccupation was with the mechanical equipment which makes merchandising and distribution far more efficient in the United States than in any other country. Mr. Korolev and his associates devoted days looking at one gadget after another. They would spend an hour or more on one dishwashing machine in a restaurant, taking copious notes on how it worked, and then go on to a potato peeler, and so on through the wonders of a modern mass-production kitchen; the next day it would be a meat-packing plant and new fascination with assembly-line meat-preparation and -packaging machines that could turn out a completely sealed pound of bacon with only the occasional attention of a mechanic.

The number one objective of Mr. Korolev, however, was a potato-chip factory. It seems that Mr. Khrushchev during his visit earlier in the year had met potato chips for the first time. Russia had a surplus of potatoes and the potato chip looked like just the thing to solve the problem. But you can't make potato chips by hand with a labor shortage. So Mr. Korolev was clearly under orders to bring back a potato-chip factory. When he was told there was no modern potato-chip factory in New York, he was suspicious and thought I was keeping him from his goal deliberately. So to satisfy his desires he was taken to one of the biggest plants in the United States — in Pennsylvania — where he bought his factory.

Judging by this experience, there must be thousands of machines which the Russians would like to adopt, ranging from automatic pea pickers to modern coal-mining monsters, from electric blenders to electronic power plant control systems, and so on. Adding up the inventive effort which has gone into developing these thousands of devices, one can readily understand the eagerness of the Russians to buy them.

Soft Soap

But the Russians have some major obstacles to overcome in increasing their imports of such products from the West. First, there is the obvious block of basic enmity. The Western nations know they are in a fight for survival in which economic strength will be a prime factor and they are not eager to contribute to Russian industrial growth.

Second, the Russians must live down a past in which they have demonstrated poor faith in a great number of agreements. A large block to trade with the United States is the unwillingness of the Russians to make a reasonable settlement for the civilian-goods portion of our wartime lend-lease aid. Some $2.6 billion of non-military goods remained in Russian hands after the war. We have offered to settle the account for $800 million but the Russians will not go above $300 million. And there has been a variety of lesser broken economic agreements involving both government and business which cast doubt upon the trustworthiness of the Russians, not to mention our dismal experience with Russian duplicity in political agreements.

Third, the Russians are famous for their disrespect of patents. They have never signed the international agreements which protect patent owners. A company which sells a patented machine to the Russians can almost take for granted that they will immediately copy it. There may be a need for 1,000 of the bacon-packaging machines I showed Mr. Korolev's team, but it is safe to assume that the Russians will never buy more than 1 from the American company that makes them. The other 999 will be made in a Russian factory after each of the American machine's parts has been painstakingly copied.

The Russians are well aware of these obstacles and have made deliberate efforts to overcome them. The initial move in the current drive to increase American exports was a letter from Khrushchev to President Eisenhower on June 2, 1958, proposing an expansion of trade between the two nations: "The Soviet Union is now engaged in carrying out a new and extensive program for a further increase in the production of consumer goods. . . . This program pursues exclusively peaceful purposes. . . ."[3] He mentioned specifically a number of harmless products, such as vending machines, but he also included some items which the United States government regards as of military value. It appears that the Russians really do want such things as potato-chip factories for peaceful use, but no one is deluded by the "consumer goods" line into thinking the Russians' first priority is not still for such things as chemicals, which have a high military priority.

To calm the fears of business about their trustworthiness, the Russians have tried an old trick, the big gesture. Ever since World War II the Soviet had owed duPont $1,500,000 for technical assistance which the chemical company had provided Russian industry. Suddenly, in 1959, with much fanfare, the Russians paid the full amount. It was, of course, no coincidence that this was at the time that they were trying to obtain more American-made goods, especially chemical equipment. Actually the Russians probably underestimated the sophistication of American businessmen and may have done themselves more harm than good by this gesture. Few businessmen saw any reason to assume there had been a basic change in Russian ways, and for many it simply served to emphasize the fact that duPont had been kept waiting over ten years for payment.

Thus the Russians have not been very effective in changing the Western image of their trading intentions and methods. But they are counting on breaking the barriers with the help of what they see as the fundamental weaknesses of capitalistic society: the profit motive and disunity. The Communists are quite convinced that if they dangle a profitable-looking deal in front of a group of businessmen one of them will jump at it. Furthermore, they assume that when one businessman jumps, the rest will start jumping because they won't want to lose out on the profits. And they follow the same strategy to the national level, playing one country off against another, looking for the weak link who will want more trade enough to close its eyes to the consequences. It is the old "divide and conquer" approach brought up-to-date in economic relations — the modern form of warfare.

The Western Response

The cynical Russian expectations have proved correct to some extent, though they have fallen short of their full objectives. There is disagreement both within the United States and among our allies as to just how much trade is justified, and the profit motive has been constantly in evidence, pushing policies beyond the edge of bounds set by sober judgment.

All are agreed that equipment of direct military value should not be exported, including not only arms but also such items as aircraft control devices which can be used for military purposes. The problems begin as we move into the area of products which, while not strictly of military use, have a clear value in adding to the war potential of the Soviet: industrial machinery, electronic devices, and the like. The United States government maintains what is known as the "Positive List" of products which are considered sufficiently valuable strategically so that they should not be shipped to the Russians. The list includes such items as synthetic rubber, alloy steels, electronic tubes, generators, and construction equipment. A company must obtain a license to export a product on the list to any country, including friendly nations, a practice necessary to control possible re-exports from other nations to the Russians. Usually licenses will not be given to export goods on the Positive List to countries inside the Iron Curtain. The volume of trade affected is indicated by the fact that products on the list make up about 10 percent of total American exports.

Our allies are committed to the same general policies as we are in the embargo of items of military value to the Russians. A Coordinating Committee (COCOM), composed of representatives of fourteen leading Western nations, works constantly on reviewing the strategic significance of individual products and attempting to bring the export control policies of the member nations into harmony. By and large, the process is successful. Reports from people who have escaped from behind the Iron Curtain testify to certain bottlenecks in the Communist war-production system due, at least in part, to inability to import strategic items. Soviet agents are known to have gone to considerable lengths to smuggle embargoed items into Russia.

But the embargo lists of all COCOM countries are not the same. The United States has consistently maintained a higher level of controls. For example, the Russians have given a high priority to completion of several steam electric power plants in eastern Russia which are to be fueled by natural gas brought in by pipeline. Their construction has been held up by lack of adequate pipe. The Russians have tried several times to buy pipe in the United States but have been turned down. They have, however, been successful in buying pipe from Germany, Italy, and France.

And even within the United States there is disagreement as to what should and should not be exported. The Kennedy administration evidently began with a desire to maintain the higher level of trade attained in 1960 as a gesture of goodwill. But the cooling of relations, after the Berlin crisis started in the summer of 1961, caused a re-evaluation of the policy, and the volume of licenses approved dropped sharply from $23.2 million in the January–March quarter to $11.6 million in the July–September quarter. It appears that the administration has no fixed concept of what should and should not be exported from a military point of view. Rather, the export control system serves as one of its bargaining weapons in the Cold War.

There is still greater division of opinion about the handling of the much larger number of products which are not on the Positive List. Our government has a long "General License Subgroup A List" of clearly nonmilitary items, such as flashlight batteries, textile machinery, grindstones, and typewriters which may be exported without control. For all other products a license must be obtained to export to Communist countries, but the government is currently quite liberal in permitting their exportation. Thus the decision to export them is largely left to the businessman.

Although the Russians would have expected under these circumstances that competitive businessmen in pursuit of profit would readily accept their offers, that has not proved true. The most notable case in point is the refusal by the American chemical industry of a $100 million proposition.[4] As we have noted, building up the Russian chemical industry has a top Russian priority. The purchase of chemical plants was mentioned prominently in Mr. Khrushchev's 1958 letter to President Eisenhower. Close on the heels of that letter came a specific proposal to purchase more than $100 million worth of equipment. Although it is possible that our government might have refused licenses for the sales, the decision was actually made by the Manufacturing Chemists' Association, speaking for the industry. When the MCA polled its members, who operate about 90 percent of the production of the American chemical industry, not one vote was cast in favor of accepting the Russian proposal.

The MCA position was based upon an assessment of the economic value to the Soviets of obtaining the chemical plants. It was estimated that 10,000 man-years of the best American technical and scientific talent had been necessary to achieve the chemical know-how embodied in those plants. If the Russians were unable to purchase the equipment, they would be forced to devote the full-time efforts of about 1,400 of their best chemists and chemical engineers to developing the processes themselves to achieve the objectives of the Seven Year Plan. That sort of effort would require a major diversion of technical manpower from other projects, slowing down the rate of economic growth and probably delaying progress in military areas requiring similar scientific personnel, such as rocket propulsion fuels and nuclear bomb development.

Reinforcing this strategic reasoning were practical considerations. The chemical group noted the Russian record of poor faith in financial dealings and its disrespect for patents. While the $100 million figure was impressive, it did not offer sufficient financial gain either for the companies or for the nation as a whole to offset the tremendous boost it would give the Russians. All told, therefore, it looked like a very poor bargain for the United States, and the MCA emphatically recommended that the United States government refuse to license any exports under the proposal and encourage our allies to do the same.

Extension of this type of resistance to our allies has proved quite difficult, however. For the United States, exports in general and business with the Russians in particular are relatively inconsequential. We could eliminate the latter, as we virtually did in the early 1950's, and hardly notice the difference. But for Europeans, trade is vital and the Russians are an important market. Their point of view is aptly described in the words of J. B. Scott, Sales Director of Crompton Parkinson Ltd., who headed the British mission to Moscow which concluded a four-year $1.12 billion trade agreement in 1954:

"We in the United Kingdom, with a population of 50 million people, can expect to feed only 30 million; we therefore must export or die. Many of our traditional and Commonwealth markets are shrinking because of local manufacture and indigenous supply, and we must look for new export outlets. In spite of their spectacular propaganda (such as hitting the moon) which demonstrate that in some fields the Soviets are ahead of us, they are, in my opinion, still 20 years behind the United Kingdom, Western Europe, and the United States. I feel, therefore, that there is a market between the Soviet Union and the United Kingdom, to speak only of my own country, which can be to the advantage of both for the next 25 years."[5]

Mr. Scott is not unmindful of the arguments against exports to Russia but he does not feel that the problem is his concern: "There are many people in the United Kingdom . . . who think it wrong to trade with Communist countries. For my own part, I say let the government be your conscience." But in a democracy, the government is collectively the people and subject to the pressures both of individual businessmen and of the basic economics which Mr. Scott describes. So the British have gone much further than we in meeting the Russian desires for manufacturing equipment. Vickers-Armstrong has sold a $6.3 million chemical plant. A group of British firms agreed to build a $39 million tire factory which Mr. Scott says "will be the most modern and up-to-date factory in Europe, with a capacity of 2 million tires a year for vehicles ranging in size and type from the smallest passenger car to the largest earth-moving machinery."

The other European countries follow much the same course. The German firm, Krupp, is delivering a $12.5 million synthetic textile plant to the Russians. Trade between Free Germany and Communist Germany adds up to $500 million per year. The Italians and Russians concluded a four-year agreement in 1957 under which trade between them has more than doubled in three years, standing now at $77 million per year. The Italians are shipping a durable cord factory, chemical plants, precision lathes, the latest equipment for textile, food, and printing industries, and other technical products. Total Western European sales to the Communist bloc in 1960 were $2.4 billion compared to $193 million from the United States.

Clearly the Russians are right in believing that the profit motive and disunity are major weaknesses in the Western defenses. In view of the European practices, any sweeping limitation upon American exports to Russia makes little sense. Our effectiveness is limited to those areas in which American technology is more advanced than that of other countries. Actually this covers a rather wide range of processes. It is generally agreed that virtually all the chemical equipment in the $100 million Russian proposal was available only from American companies. Thus in turning down that bid our chemical industry was able to cut the Russians off from a major source of technological progress. The plants they have obtained from the European countries will give them a part of what they wanted, but they must still devote their own technical effort to further advances if they want to achieve their goal of a chemical industry second to none.

The Communists can therefore claim substantial success in their effort to expedite their economic progress by drawing upon the know-how of the West. We are able to deprive them of our most advanced technology and products of direct military value. But we are handing over to them thousands of man-years of technological know-how in everything from synthetic-fiber plants to potato-chip factories.

Paying the Bill

One might hope that in return for this boost to the Soviet economy the West were receiving comparable gains from its trade with the Russians. In fact, Russian exports seem to be responsible for as much consternation as gain among Western business circles. The Communists have been accused of selling oil and other products at low prices to disrupt world markets, and many people are convinced that their exports are primarily directed by political motives. This conclusion is not, however, accurate. Political considerations do play some part in Russian exporting, but economic necessity is the major element. The Russians would like to be able to obtain their imports without losing anything in the process. In his 1958 letter Mr. Khrushchev said that the Russians hoped to buy against "credits and payments in installments." But the United States government has no intention of financing exports to Russia and, under the Johnson Act of 1934, private American business is forbidden to extend long-term credits to any nation which has defaulted on obligations to the United States. The Russians have defaulted on payment of $573 million of World War I debt of the Czarist government which they are most unlikely to pay. Likewise our allies, despite their desires for Russian trade, insist on immediate payments. Mr. Scott, for example, despite his eagerness to expand trade, emphasized that "there can be no question of a government to government loan. Such a loan is quite unthinkable in view of the many underdeveloped territories of the world."[6]

So Russia must pay for its imports. It does have large gold resources but mining gold is costly. The deposits are in the arctic north. With decreasing use of forced labor in Russia, it is harder to get men to work the deposits and, whether free or forced, manpower used to mine gold is not available for other forms of production. Hence, while they do pay for some imports with gold, the Russians have generally preferred to export other products which represent less internal expenditure of effort. So far as possible they limit their exports to raw materials of which domestic production is ample, with manufactured goods sold only in limited amounts, chiefly to the underdeveloped countries.

Russian exports to the United States have ranged between $10 million and $40 million since World War II. About one third of the total is accounted for by benzene, a coal-tar product of which Russia happens to have a surplus, filling a United States need. Otherwise our imports from Russia are an assortment of items which are of little consequence to our economy: meat and sausage casings, fish and fish products, undressed furs, fertilizers, photographic goods, books, and handicrafts. Some of these imports might be increased. The volume of fur imports is severely restricted by exclusion of ermine, fox, mink, and several other types under a section of the Trade Agreements Act adopted when it was renewed in 1951. This section is a bit of protection which the domestic fur producers put through with the help of the strong anti-Russian sentiment at the time of the Korean War. Russian crab meat is excluded under a section of the Tariff Act of 1930, which prohibits the importation of a product manufactured by forced labor. The Soviets say that forced labor is not used but they will not permit on-the-spot investigation to verify their claim.

In his letter to President Eisenhower, Mr. Khrushchev proposed that increased American exports should be paid for by Russian exports of a number of raw materials, such as manganese and chrome ores. But the United States has no interest in importing these products from Russia. We obtain our imports now from friendly nations, chrome ore from Turkey, manganese from Brazil, and so forth. It would be poor policy to switch our purchases from these countries to Russia. In the first place, it would weaken us strategically because it would make us dependent upon a highly unreliable source. In the second place, it would be a sharp economic blow to our allies for whom exports of raw materials to us are a prime source of income.

From time to time, the Russians have caused a minor flurry by bringing some manufactured goods into the United States. In 1959, for example, a few much-publicized shipments of scientific educational equipment were made through the Ealing Corp. of Cambridge, Massachusetts. The microscopes and other items were of excellent quality and the prices were well below those of competitive American products. But the flow of equipment has not continued and the Russians do not seem inclined to make a regular practice of exporting manufactured goods in volume to the United States.

With the exception of the benzene, therefore, Russian exports to the United States are not important as specific supplements to our economy nor in total volume.

In Europe the story is quite different. Just as Russia is a valuable market for Western European exports, so it is also a useful source of a number of raw materials in which the industrialized countries are deficient. Britain can look to Russia for grain, timber, manganese, pig iron, and assorted other products. Italy is obtaining the same sort of products and in addition buying about 15 percent of its oil from Russia at lower prices than it has to pay for oil from the Middle East. Thus, while these countries are giving Russia more in the way of valuable machinery and equipment, they are also receiving more in return than the United States receives.

But the mutually advantageous exports of raw materials which Russia has worked out with European countries under trade agreements are not sufficient to pay for her imports. Therefore, the Russians have had to find other ways to increase their exports, and this has led to the bargain-price sales which have often been interpreted as politically motivated. In 1957, for example, the Russians caused much consternation by selling tin and aluminum in the London market at 10 to 20 percent below the going world market prices. This move was widely interpreted as an attempt to disrupt the free world's economic system. However, in 1957, Russia was running a sizable deficit in its balance of payments with the British Commonwealth sterling area, notably for imports of rubber from Malaya and wool from South Africa; hence it badly needed British pounds. Sales of tin and aluminum, which were in surplus supply in the Communist bloc, filled the need.

The prices may have been set so low in part for political disruption purposes, but the experts surmise that the Russians were primarily interested in making sure that the sales were made.[7] They were trying to unload large quantities of tin and aluminum and they didn't want to take any chances on not selling them. In any case, knowing how free markets operate, it is quite likely that a sudden increase in supply would have caused the prices to drop anyway. So the Russians, in setting a low price initially, were probably simply anticipating the inevitable.

We can therefore attribute to practical economic motivations the main patterns of Russian trade: the desire to obtain technology and raw materials essential for industrial expansion and an expanding industrial complex and the necessity to sell products to pay for these imports. But this is not to say that politics do not play a part in Russian international trade.

The Political Overtones

To bring the political aspects of the Soviet trade policies into focus we have to add to the picture the Communist objectives in their economic relations with the less-developed nations. Their ultimate goal, of course, is domination of each country. The immediate steps to be taken to this end are (1) to create a favorable impression of themselves and (2) to weaken the economic and political systems which support the West. By skillful and opportunistic actions the Communists have used their economic aid and trade to very good advantage for these purposes.

Russian economic aid has been small by comparison with that of the United States, running around $200 million per year against our roughly $1.6 billion. But they have tried to make each ruble count to maximum advantage. They have concentrated on conspicuous projects which will receive public acclaim. In Afghanistan, while the United States concentrated on a badly needed irrigation, hydroelectric project in remote hills, the Russians paved the main street of the capital, Kabul, putting up a huge sign "This road was paved — courtesy of the USSR — your partner and fellow pioneer in the struggle to tame nature." The great High Aswan Dam in Egypt, a steel plant in India, and a hospital in Burma are other typical conspicuous Russian aid projects.

But from the trading point of view, the method of financing is more significant. While a large portion of United States aid has been in the form of outright grants (gifts), the Russians have stuck almost entirely to loans. Their terms are very favorable. The interest is low, usually 2.5 percent, and repayment may be made over a long period and in commodities which the country produces. The Egyptians, for example, will pay for the help in building the Aswan Dam by shipping cotton to Russia for many years to come. This system has been quite effective, partly because accepting a loan overcomes the humiliation which many countries feel at receiving hand-outs and partly because the countries are anxious to sell their raw-material output. The Egyptians were happy to have an assured market for their cotton, especially in view of the uncertainties in trading relations with European countries in the wake of the struggle which followed the seizure of the Suez Canal in 1956. They felt that the Russians had given them a good economic deal. Thus the Communists scored two gains: in spreading their propaganda and in weaning the Egyptians away from trade with the West and into their own economic orbit.

In their trading with the underdeveloped countries, the Russians have followed this same approach. The products they have purchased have usually been ones they needed for their own economy, but they have also picked their sources with a sharp eye to political advantage. Cocoa has been in short supply in Russia for some years, but it was not until Ghana became free and a prime target for Russian Communist subversion that imports became sizable. The greater supply of chocolate fits nicely as a part of the Russian effort to give the people a few more consumer goods, and the purchases from Ghana are vital in strengthening Soviet influence there and weakening Ghana's ties with the West.

After World War II, Russia almost moved Iceland into its camp with similar astute trading. Iceland must live by fishing. But the British embargoed Icelandic fish imports because of a dispute over fishing grounds, and the New England fishing industry impeded imports here by instigating Tariff Commission hearings to have tariffs raised. The Russians moved quickly, offering to buy all the fish Icelanders could catch. The people might well have fallen completely into the Russian orbit if the Hungarian rebellion had not come along to open their eyes to the way the Russians treat their satellites.

Similar political objectives seem to be behind some of the Russian exports of raw materials. As we noted above, most of these sales have been necessary to earn foreign exchange to pay for imports. In some instances, on the other hand, political designs seem to be significant. For example, in 1961 Russia proposed to sell petroleum to India for 10 percent less than the price being charged by the existing sources of crude oil in the Persian Gulf. The Communists also proposed to accept payment in Indian export commodities, such as jute. This may have been just another attempt to gain income, but it did have the clear and probably anticipated effect of embarrassing the international oil companies and, through them, the West. The Indian government did not force the companies who operate the refineries in India to buy crude oil from the Russians, but the companies were put in the position of having to cut their prices 11 percent, providing a propaganda coup for the Russians in India. And in the Middle East, a cut in prices means a cut in royalty income for the governments of Kuwait, Saudi Arabia, and other nations whose friendship the West seeks to hold. The Russians got some of the blame for the cut in income, but the Western oil companies bore the direct brunt of criticism for not holding the price line against Russian pressure.

The Soviets have also on occasion purchased products abroad

for political reasons even though they did not need them. When Argentina was hard-pressed for petroleum a few years ago, Russia stepped in and filled the need from its ample supplies, taking payment in wool and other raw materials of which Argentina had an excess supply. At the time, Russia was apparently trying to reduce its imports of wool and to manage on domestic supplies. But the opportunity to gain favorable propaganda from the Argentine crisis was considered worth the cost.

The record of success of the Russian program of aid and trade is impressive, but it may be approaching a stage where the rate of return diminishes. Much of the success has been due to the limited size and area of coverage. As the Soviet activities broaden they encounter conflicts and problems which lessen their effectiveness. For example, when they purchase products that they don't need themselves, they have sometimes felt it economically necessary to sell them abroad. But this means competing directly with the original supplier in export markets and creates resentment. The Soviets have such a problem with the cotton they have accepted in their agreement with the Egyptians. For some years Russia has produced enough cotton to be a net exporter. Egyptian cotton has therefore been re-exported into European markets at prices below the going level in competition with Egypt's direct exports.[8] This is undoubtedly one factor in the cooling of Egyptian feelings toward Russia.

A similar situation developed in Southeast Asia, when Burma exchanged shipments of rice for manufactured goods from the Red Chinese. The Chinese, of course, needed the rice for their underfed population. But they had an even greater need for imports for industrial use. So they resold the Burmese rice to Ceylon for cash. At the time there was an oversupply of rice in the world. Ceylon was a regular market for Burma and the Chinese were therefore cutting the Burmese out of potential export income.

As the Russians try to exert influence in an ever-broadening sphere they are also finding themselves caught more often in the conflicts of interests among nations. Their maneuvers in international oil have so far been fairly minor, Russian exports accounting for only about 5 percent of world oil trade. They have won favor for Russia in Italy, India, and other consuming countries without major cost to the producers. But they have already trod on the toes of the Middle Eastern nations, some of which they have been trying to win as allies. If their tactics weaken the world price still further, they can expect strong reactions from other oil-producing countries, such as Venezuela and Indonesia. Likewise, the shifting political sands of the Middle East confront the Reds with embarrassing conflicts. The conspicuous aid for the Aswan Dam is something of an albatross to the Russians as they try to win over the Iraqis and especially the Syrians, who have forcefully broken away from Nasser's control.

But the increasing hazards of Russian economic relations in no way diminish the problem which their trading activities pose for the United States. It is quite apparent that the Soviets stand ready and able to take advantage of every opportunity, and we must therefore be scrupulous in the conduct of our trading relations. The effort to raise the tariff against Icelandic fish imports is but one example of the openings we can give the Russians. Another developed in Chile in 1958. President Ibáñez was about to leave for a state visit to the United States when the United States government announced that a copper tariff, which had been suspended for some years, was to be reimposed. Copper is the main source of Chile's income, and this was a rude blow. Ibáñez canceled his trip and anti-American feeling boiled up. Alert to the situation, the Russians and the East Germans were on the spot quickly with offers to buy Chilean copper wire.

Potentials for similar propaganda coups are found in virtually every underdeveloped country today because raw materials are generally in excess supply and prices have been falling. The United States has been sharply criticized for the loss of income these countries have suffered recently, and the Russians have played up this criticism as well as their own efforts to help by buying surpluses. Add to this the protectionist drives by American producers of oil, lead, zinc, and other minerals, and we have the makings of widespread propaganda gains for the Russians.

In the Front Lines of the Cold War

The various facets of East-West trade are all vital parts of the Cold War. In them we can see very clearly the single-minded, forceful actions of the Communist machine pitted against the profit-directed, multibodied system of our free, private enterprise society. The results to date are not reassuring. It is hard to escape the conclusion that the machinery and equipment exported to the Russians are far more valuable to them than the materials the West has received in return. Despite a few tactical errors in selling imported goods, the Russians seem to be highly effective in terms of both economics and propaganda in their trading in raw materials with the less-developed countries. In both forms of trade, we must admit that the profit motive is proving more of an Achilles heel than a sinew of strength. The drive to maximize sales of manufactured products, the problems of open-market pricing of raw materials, and the pressures for protection of domestic industries by tariffs all stand out as prime weaknesses of which the Russians are taking advantage.

In a democratic society it is not easy to remedy such weaknesses. There is no one point at which we can correct the problem. It does little good to say that the Speed-Feed Company should not sell its tool-changing devices to the Russians, for there are thousands of equally significant decisions made by other Americans, not to mention the thousands made by men like Mr. Scott in other countries. The man who made the final decision to reimpose the copper tariff is not a traitor even though his action clearly aided the enemy.

The problem, rather, is one of a national state of mind. Our individual actions and our government policies are all part of a total attitude. We have not yet as a nation decided to make anything like a total commitment to winning the Cold War. The Russians have made that commitment, devoting their every action to the single-minded purpose of world domination. We and our allies are still hoping that we can get by with a few sacrifices while essentially continuing to live by the old ways of free enterprise and liberal world trade.

■■■■■■■■■■■ 8

The
Lingering Curse
of Exploitation

"Blood-Sucking United States Capitalists" — "The Long, Greedy Arm of Wall Street"

Such characterizations of American overseas investors make effective communist propaganda slogans, for they find a receptive audience in much of the world. Throughout the underdeveloped countries capitalism is second only to colonialism as a whipping boy. Large portions of the population think of our businessmen as "exploiters" extracting big profits at the expense of poorly paid local workers and draining off the wealth of the land with dividends and exports of valuable resources. This is a heavy handicap for American business to bear in its efforts abroad, and a substantial drag on our whole foreign policy. It is important, therefore, to examine critically the substance of the charges and to do what we can about minimizing them.

The Dark Past

The seeds of the exploitive reputation were planted in the early phases of American overseas investments around the turn of the century. Most of our first foreign operations were extractive or agricultural ventures which became the targets of bitter criticism. Although each situation was unique in some way, the main sources of animosity were much the same in every instance. A brief history of one prominent example, the Mexican oil investments, will therefore shed light on the whole problem.

The Mexican oil story starts with Porfirio Díaz, who governed

120

Mexico as virtual dictator from 1876 to 1910. Díaz came to power in a country torn by fifty years of political turmoil, economically poor, and underdeveloped. He stabilized the political situation and attacked the problem of economic development directly and energetically. He saw that, lacking internal financial resources, Mexico needed foreign capital and that, without a developed internal market, the country's growth would have to start with what it had — its natural resources. Foreign investors were leery of Mexico because of its revolutionary history; hence Díaz needed to offer some carrots.

The chief concession was a constitutional amendment in 1884 by which the owners of surface properties were declared to be the owners of petroleum reserves under their property. Prior to that time, all subsurface mineral resources were the property of the state, the common practice in countries of Spanish origin, and they could not be sold to individuals. Resources in this situation could be extracted only by concession. In addition, Díaz helped the petroleum companies with tax reductions, controls over labor, and other practical measures aimed at increasing profits and reducing risks and complications.

These carrots were sufficient to entice several American and British oil companies to make substantial investments in Mexico, especially from 1900 to 1910. Meantime, the Mexican people had grown restive under Díaz's stern rule and in 1910 he was thrown out. Many Mexicans considered that the granting of property rights to the oil companies was unconstitutional, and the new constitution of 1917 returned the rights to the government. During the next twenty years the government engaged in a bitter legal fight with the oil companies, trying to regain control over the properties. The United States government in general supported the oil industry with forceful diplomacy.

In 1937, the petroleum labor unions demanded large wage increases and other concessions including the right to name men for a number of supervisory positions. A bitter strike ensued, culminating in the expropriation of the oil properties by order of President Lazaro Cárdenas in 1938. Underlying this dispute were strong feelings about working conditions, which Cárdenas described thus vividly:

> What center of oil production does not have its private
> police force for protection of private, selfish, and often

illegal interests? These organizations, whether authorized by the Government or not, are guilty of innumerable outrages, abuses and murders, always on behalf of the companies that employ them.

Who is not aware of the irritating difference between the housing facilities in the company fields? Comfort for the foreign personnel; misery, drabness, and insalubrity for the Mexicans. Refrigeration and protection against tropical insects for the former; indifference and neglect, and always grudgingly given medical service and drugs for the latter; lower wages and harder, more exhausting labor for our people.[1]

Cárdenas may have colored his description somewhat, but objective observers confirm the main elements; more important, this is the image which the Mexican population as a whole believed, for Cárdenas was their hero.

Although few of the early overseas investments actually ended in the catastrophe of expropriation, their evolution and the consequent bitterness of feelings have usually followed much the same pattern. It is hard to condemn the American investors because what they did seemed essentially right and sound at the time. The initial government concessions were a *sine qua non*, essential to attract investment into large and risky ventures. They were acts of responsible governments which the investors assumed would be honored in the future. The governments needed foreign capital to do a job. The capital came, and it did the job reasonably well — creating employment, earning income for the country, and setting the process of economic development going. Although some companies probably made a killing, most seem to have earned quite moderate profits. For example, from 1899 to 1955 the United Fruit Company earned an average profit of 13 percent per year on the investment in its great banana operations in Central and South America.[2] The rate was higher in the earlier part of the period but, considering the risks, a 20 to 25 percent return would not be considered excessive. The oil companies in Mexico calculated their annual profits from 1934 to 1936 at 8 percent of investment, and even the Mexican government only claimed they were making 17 percent.[3]

On the labor side, the treatment was usually good by local standards. The "misery, drabness, and insalubrity" described by Cárdenas have been the common lot of the working classes in underdeveloped countries for centuries, and only very recently has a small portion begun to rise above that level. The American companies offered at least a little more than the average peon had had. Most Mexicans even in the 1930's had little chance to get medical services or drugs, so even if the "grudgingly given" charge were true, Cárdenas' own comments verify the relatively better status of the oil workers. There seems little doubt that there were cases of real abuse in the handling of workers, especially in the 1880's and 1890's. The most extensively documented history of Mexican mining reports a number of incidents ranging from high-handed treatment to outright brutality.[4] Again, however, the actions of American companies overseas appear to have been no harsher than those of native employers nor, indeed, much worse than those of American business at home in the same era. The early history of the mining industry in the western United States is replete with stories of brutal repression by company police and tough strikebreaking tactics.[5] The unpleasant truth is that it was not until this century that managements generally learned to deal with labor in a humane manner.

The luxurious facilities for the Americans in foreign camps were an unfortunate but practical necessity. There were insufficient qualified technical and managerial personnel in the host countries; hence Americans had to be imported, and they would not come without good living conditions. There was no deliberate attempt to flaunt the luxury before the local workers. The contrast in living standards was a natural reflection of the difference in supply of the two groups of employees and, in fact, was duplicated in the local population itself. That is, the extremes between American managers and Mexican oil workers were no greater than those between the Mexican managerial class and the general population. The companies may be criticized for not bringing more Mexicans into their management organization. Integration at this level would have emphasized that the difference in standard of living was a management-worker distinction, not an American-Mexican one. But even this would have been difficult to accomplish, for few Mexicans had the necessary technical or managerial skills, and the educated Mexicans were not favorably disposed to life in the relatively raw oil camps as compared with the amenities of Mexico City.

Thus there was nothing in this situation which one can single out as evil or malicious. But that does not change the fact that it created an image of exploitation. The logics I have outlined meant nothing to the typical Mexican peon. He knew only a few key facts: Mexican resources were being shipped out of his country, an American company was making a profit, the American employees were living like kings, and he was still eking out only a bare existence. That, to him, was exploitation.

A New Era

The Mexican oil expropriations were a tremendous shock to American overseas business. They were a key turning point in the evolution of management methods. Many executives had already been thinking of new approaches as they sensed the changing environment abroad, but the expropriations drove the lesson home. It was quite clear that even though past policies might not have been strictly culpable, they were a failure, for any policy which ends in disaster is a failure. A new approach which went out to meet the "exploitation" criticism with positive, constructive efforts was needed.

Indicative of the progressive management which has evolved from this line of thinking are the policies of the Creole Petroleum Corporation, the subsidiary of Standard Oil Company (New Jersey) in Venezuela, which have been described in a study by the National Planning Association.[6] A summary of these policies conveys a vivid picture of a company seeking in a variety of ways to satisfy the feelings of the people and make itself a good citizen of the country (the NPA report was written in 1955; the data given here are updated to 1961):

1. Every effort is made to employ Venezuelans at all levels. Virtually all workers are of local origin; despite a serious shortage of technical personnel in the country, 57 percent of the staff are local nationals and even 29 percent of the executives are Venezuelans, including three of the eight members of the Board of Directors. There is an extensive recruiting, training, and scholarship program designed to increase the number of Venezuelans in the higher levels.

2. Creole, in conjunction with other oil companies, has contributed substantial sums to the American International Association, which undertakes demonstration and training programs in agriculture, education, and public health in Venezuela.

3. At various times Creole has lent money to Venezuelan enterprises in food production, dredging, and other fields to assist their

development, and it purchases half of its supplies in Venezuela (about $19 million per year).

4. It provides workers with quarters which are not extravagant but definitely superior by local standards, including ample room, plumbing, and such services as trash disposal. To build independence, efforts are being made to facilitate the purchase of homes by the workers.

5. Excellent schools and hospitals are provided, as well as recreational facilities.

6. At the outset, because of the isolation of oil camps, the company itself had to build and manage all facilities from sanitation to schools. To improve political and social relations, it has started a program of community integration designed to turn over increasing responsibility for public facilities to the camp residents. The residents are encouraged to form organizations with which Creole can work on school administration, camp facilities, and similar problems. The organizations are now largely consultative, but the objective is to turn over actual management of local affairs to them.

The Creole story is not typical inasmuch as it is one of the most progressive companies in these matters. At the opposite end of the spectrum there are still a few companies that resort to harsh labor relations and other means which deserve censure as exploitive. But the great majority of American companies are seriously trying to live down the past with efforts like those of Creole.

Policies of this nature have set an entirely different tone for the relations with the people and governments of host countries. But the curse of "exploitation" is by no means removed, especially where its origins are deeply set in the dark past. For example, even though United Fruit Company has made a concerted effort to raise wages and to improve the schools, housing, and other facilities for its workers, the company is still treated with cold dislike and very few politicians in Central America will say a kind word about it. The lot of the mining and petroleum companies is especially hard because the charge that they are extracting the wealth of the country remains, no matter how much they work to develop progressive policies in labor and other matters.

Companies in manufacturing and trade have had an easier row to hoe, partly because they do not encounter this "extracting" problem and partly because they did not become a major factor until after the lessons of the oil expropriations had been learned. But the "exploitation" label has still been hung on them, chiefly for two reasons: their competitive status and their remissions of profits.

Someone Gets Hurt

The competitive question revolves around the charge that American business uses its superior size and other resources to exploit foreign markets at the expense of local business. This issue is, of course, a concern primarily among local business circles and thus is not as broad a source of criticism as that of labor exploitation. However, "business circles" in many instances cover quite a wide segment of the population. For example, Sears, Roebuck in Mexico has periodically been threatened with restrictions sought by the masses of little tradesmen in Mexico.[7] Sears has introduced a number of practices which put pressure on the small merchant. It established a single price system, which contrasted with the traditional price haggling, as well as high standards of uniform quality control compared with the erratic quality of many local sources, and mass merchandising, which has permitted lower prices for some products; moreover, its advertising was expert. The merchants responded with a strong movement in the Mexican Chamber of Commerce for restrictions against new investments by foreign capital in commerce. The government, wishing to encourage foreign investment in general, has fended off these efforts, but the threat hangs over the heads of Sears and other American investors in the field.

Similar resistance lies behind the difficulties of Singer Manufacturing Company in Japan.[8] After World War II, Singer was not allowed to import sewing machines into Japan. When it tried to enter the market by buying a half interest in a Japanese firm in 1954, a storm of protest arose. There were a few large Japanese manufacturers, but much of the production came from hundreds of small producers, who ran little shops and farmed out jobs to people who worked in their homes. An estimated 300,000 Japanese families were dependent upon the industry, a considerable portion of them in the small workshops. These people saw in the financial and technological strength of Singer a major threat to their existence. Singer in a single factory would turn out better machines with a few workers, replacing a mass of home and small shop operations. Singer's proposal became a major national issue and the politically sensitive government refused to give approval. Singer went ahead with the investment because it felt it had to establish itself in the market, but without government approval it could not obtain dollars to send earnings home to the parent company.

Opposition such as Sears and Singer have encountered is hard to answer because the threat to the local enterprises is real. Foreign governments are generally anxious to bring in American business exactly because it has capacities which are not locally available. Sometimes these capacities are not a threat to local vested interests — for example, chemical operations which bring completely new technologies. But usually there will be at least a few people whose livelihood is dependent upon a business which may be replaced by the new methods, and sometimes, as with Sears and Singer, the number affected may be quite large.

The compensating factors are in benefits to the country as a whole and to the people directly involved in the new operations. For example, Sears's quality control, single pricing, and lower costs have all directly helped the Mexican consumer. Sears obtains over 80 percent of its products from more than 1,300 Mexican suppliers. Many of these are relatively small factories to which Sears has given financial and technical help. For example, it brought American production men down to help a shoe factory cut costs, and it lent money to a woman dressmaker who had two sewing machines so that she could expand to an eighteen-machine shop. And the company's employment practices have won it a high ranking in desirability as an employer. Good pay is only part of the story. The company has given superior opportunities and treatment to Mexicans. For example, in most Mexican department stores, each clerk is trusted with only part of a transaction — one starts the sale and a cashier completes it. Sears introduced the American practice of having one clerk complete the whole job, thus enhancing the clerk's sense of importance.

Who Profits?

The remission of profits arouses resentment because of the shortage of foreign exchange, which is still a major problem in the underdeveloped countries. The crying need in these countries is to import machinery and industrial materials to build up their economies. To divert dollar exchange from this use for the payment of dividends by American subsidiaries seems a wasteful sacrifice. This concern is understandable in view of the large portion of the supply of foreign exchange which goes into payment of profits in such instances as the following (the figures are for 1960):

Country	Imports from United States (millions of dollars)	Payments to United States for investment income (millions of dollars)
Australia	$387	$37
Brazil	427	45
Mexico	810	65

A notable instance of this problem is the General Motors operation in Australia mentioned in Chapter 1. GM's Holden car has been highly successful. For many years the company piled up profits, which it plowed back into expansion of its operations. Eventually Holden reached the stage where it wished to start returning profits to the parent company, its dividends reached $18 million in 1959, a large enough factor in Australia's balance of payments to attract frequent critical comment from the Australian press and public.

This is another one of those unfortunate situations in which condemnation is based on one surface fact whereas the full facts tell a quite different story. Taken by itself, the $18 million looks like quite a loss to the Australian economy. But there are two major offsetting factors which more than make up for it.

First, there is the contribution to over-all Australian economic growth which resulted from GM's initial decision to manufacture the Holden and its steady reinvestment of profits. By 1959 the total output of the operation had risen to $260 million per year. The greater portion of the income from this output was for the benefit of Australians: 54 percent to suppliers, 20 percent to employees, 10.5 percent for taxes, and 8.5 percent of depreciation and retained profits used to build the business. Only 7 percent was taken out of the economy as dividends. The profit is a good one but not out of line as compensation for the risks of the initial venture and the contributions of GM technical knowledge and management skill which have added an important increment to the whole Australian economy.

The second point is the net impact on the balance of payments. Before GM started manufacturing in 1948, all motor vehicles had to be imported, so that all expenditures for vehicles had to come out of the supply of foreign exchange. In 1947 only 50,000 trucks and cars were imported into Australia — about all the limited foreign exchange resources would permit. By starting manufacture, GM made it possible for Australians to obtain far more vehicles within their foreign exchange resources. Dividends paid by Holden to GM take some foreign exchange. But with these dividends running at 7 percent of sales, the Australians can obtain about fourteen times as many vehicles as they would be able to import with the same amount of foreign exchange. In 1959 Holden delivered $260 million worth of vehicles while requiring only $18 million of foreign exchange. If all the vehicles had been imported, $150 million to $200 million more foreign exchange would have been needed, the exact amount depending on how much local expenditure for advertising and other costs was involved. The availability of local production has permitted the country to divert a considerable amount of foreign exchange which might have been needed for vehicle imports into the purchase of other imports, industrial machinery, raw materials, and so on. Thus, although it appears at first glance that the GM dividends are a drain of foreign exchange, in fact, they are a fraction of the much greater saving of foreign exchange which they have created to the benefit of Australia.

The Balance of Benefits

As the essence of the "exploitation" question is whether American business benefits at the expense of foreign economies, it is helpful to look at the over-all impact of our investments upon an area. The U.S. Department of Commerce has provided such a picture in a broad study of the operations of American companies accounting for 90 percent of our investments in Latin America.[9] We can divide the operations into the two main categories whose economic characteristics are different: primary material producers, and manufacturing enterprises.

The chief economic function of the primary material producers (Figure 23) is the generation of income from the resources of the country — metals, petroleum, food products, and so on. There are those abroad who criticize the mere idea of exporting unreplaceable resources, such as minerals, but this position is not realistic. If these countries are to progress rapidly, they must import machinery and other products they cannot now manufacture. Food exports alone do not bring in enough income, and oil and minerals are their only other large marketable assets. Also, their deposits of the products they are exporting are generally so plentiful that hoarding them for future domestic use makes no sense — how would Venezuela ever use all its oil? or Chile, all its copper? Furthermore, there is a distinct possibility that technological progress may render the resources less valuable in the future. New fuels and materials could displace much of the demand for these raw materials. So this

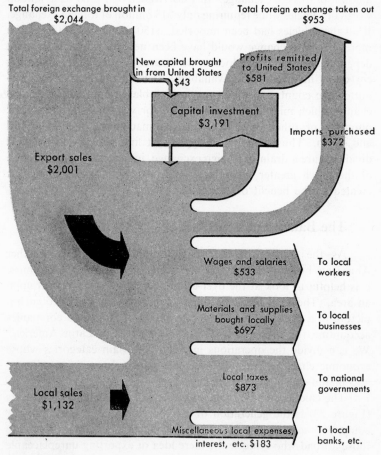

FIG. 23   Flow of income and expenditures of United States-owned Latin-American primary material producers, 1955 (in millions of dollars).

argument has little meaning, and the real issue is whether the countries are getting a fair share of the proceeds from the exports.

The figures show that the remissions of dollars by the American companies took $581 million or 29 percent of the $2,001 million earned from the exports of primary products. In evaluating this figure we must bear in mind that only part of it is profits. A mine or an oil well is a wasting asset for the owner. He makes an initial investment and then his "profits" are both a recovery of the value of his investment and true profits. If he invests $1,000 in a mine which operates for five years, he must earn $1,500 in all if he expects a 10 percent profit — $1,000 to recover his capital and $100 per year profit. Thus a substantial portion of the "profit" is in fact return of capital. The book value of the investments at the time of the study was $3,191 million; hence allowing a reasonable amount for return of capital, the rate of profit on investment was in the range of 10 to 15 percent. Considering the risks involved, this would not appear excessive. The importation of supplies and equipment for the operations required $372 million of foreign exchange, of which $43 million was supplied by new capital, leaving a net of $329 million to be met from the proceeds of the exports, about 16 percent of the total.

That leaves 53 percent of the export income as a net gain for the host countries from which they benefit in two ways. First, it is a major source of foreign exchange to finance imports. Exports by these American companies provided in all about 30 percent of the foreign exchange earnings of the Latin-American countries. In practical terms this means that if the American companies or other foreign investors had not put their money into building the exports of oil, copper, bananas, and the like, the Latin Americans would have had to get along with about one-third less of the machine tools, chemicals, electrical equipment, and so on, that they want so badly, for their own resources were too limited to make the investments. Second, the income has played an important role in the internal economies of Latin America, providing wages for workers, purchases for local suppliers, and so on.

The role of the manufacturing operations (Figure 24) lies in saving foreign exchange and developing the internal economy. One cannot say precisely how much foreign exchange they have saved. Undoubtedly some products are being made internally that would never have been imported — soap, for example. But observation of the nature of new manufacturing investments indicates that a large portion do replace imports, a point developed in Chapter 1. Time and again it is the story of a factory set up to supply refrigerators or automobiles or drugs or some other product which can no longer be imported. So it is fair to say that a large portion of the $1,418 million of manufactured goods sold locally would have had to be imported if the American operations were not there. The $59 million required for dividends is therefore but a small portion of the amount saved.

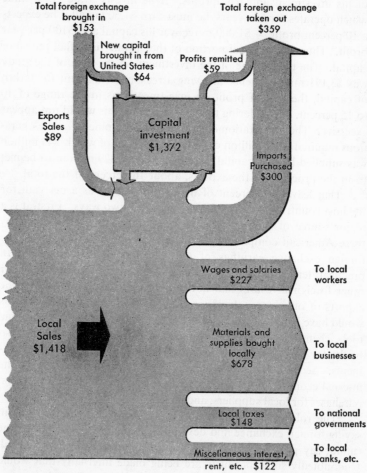

FIG. 24. Flow of income and expenditures of United States-owned manufacturing operations in Latin America, 1955 (in millions of dollars).

The internal impact of these operations on the Latin-American countries is, of course, the very essence of the industrial revolution which has set them on the road from relatively primitive levels to a new way of life in the past half century. It may be, as we shall consider in the next chapter, that American business plays too prominent a role in their manufacturing industries, but the fact is that, without the tremendous infusion of American capital, manufacturing in Latin America would be far below its present level. The $227 million of direct wage payments indicated in Figure 24 covering the employment of some 624,000 workers, are important. But even more important are the $678 million of purchases of local materials and supplies which fan out in the economies and multiply into many more jobs and purchases. When Kaiser set up a jeep factory in Argentina, for example, its purchases of equipment, parts, materials, and even office supplies gave a boost to a myriad of Argentine companies and thus to the whole economy. One more measure of the significance of these operations is the fact that new American investments accounted for about 10 percent of all new private investment in the Latin-American countries in 1955. The profits which the companies have extracted from the economies amount to only about 4 percent of the total income they have generated — certainly a fair return.

A Tough Selling Job

The logics against the "exploitive" label are strong. Although in the past there may have been abuses, by and large, overseas managers are now conscientious in their efforts to do well by their workers and help their host countries. The economic contributions to the foreign exchange earnings and internal economies far outweigh the profits gained from the investments.

But logics are one thing and changing national sentiments quite another. The memory of the less enlightened early years of American investments is firmly rooted. It is compounded by strong emotions of nationalism and dark suspicions that the United States would like to keep underdeveloped countries in a subservient economic status as a source of cheap raw materials and an outlet for manufactured exports. Furthermore, American business overseas must bear the onus of association with local capitalists whose practices are often far short of the enlightened concepts of our own country.

In a perceptive analysis, *Can Capitalism Compete?* Raymond Miller observes: "It is tragic but true that much of the business world in 'developing' countries looks upon 40 percent profit from investment and 60 percent profit from land rents as being the reward due the capitalist. . . . The world wants to move away from the iniquitous local money lender and 'exploitive capitalism.' "[10] From these roots arises the anticapitalist, socialist thinking which bears down on American business as well as on local entrepreneurs.

These assorted feelings are an ever-present sword of Damocles hanging over the head of our investments abroad. The risks of expropriation are probably not great in most instances, though we have seen in Cuba that they are by no means past. For some companies, such as United Fruit in Central America, they will doubtless remain a threat for some time to come. The problems for most overseas operations, however, are the less dramatic but still troublesome assortment of harassments and pressures from governments and labor.

Taxes may be raised, squeezing profits. The oil-producing companies are seeing this happen. Most of them started out with agreements to give 40 percent or so of their profits to the host governments. Then there was a wave of unilateral revisions after World War II establishing a 50-50 division. Now the Indonesians have decreed that their government shall get 60 percent; similar revisions are coming in other countries.

Labor unions with strong government support may extract concessions that render profitable operations impossible. The mining companies in Mexico have been caught in such a situation for twenty five years, with costs forced steadily up and no way out because of high production taxes (based on tons of ore mined) which the government will not modify. They have responded by cutting investments so that mine production has not increased, but existing operations can only keep plodding along with minimal returns.

Price controls may be administered so that companies cannot keep up with the inflation rampant in many countries. American firms selling drugs, tires, gasoline, and similar products in which broad public interest is a major factor have been the chief victims of price squeezes of this nature.

Other problems involve difficulties in bringing in American technicians, pressures for still greater local manufacture, and so on. Rarely is any one problem sufficient to wreck an operation; but in combination they do squeeze profits, hamper development, and generally deter the potential dynamic contributions of private enterprise.

Because the origins of these problems are diffused through the ranks of labor, government officials, competitors, and the population as a whole, they are not susceptible to any single direct corrective action. Rather, they call for a broad, persistent attack. A continuing effort is needed to eliminate the "exploitive" image of American business by breaking down the emotional prejudices and getting across the story of the real contributions made to host economies.

A great variety of approaches to this job have been suggested and many have made substantial progress. The National Planning Association has sponsored a series of ten pamphlets on *United States Business Performance Abroad* which tell the stories of individual companies, such as that of Creole cited earlier. These have been circulated abroad and we can hope they have had an impact on the literate, leader class at least. A number of American businesses have formed the Business Council for International Understanding (BCIU), which is bent on improving understanding and creating a better image of American business abroad. It has made some broad efforts in conjunction with the State Department, and on the local level has done such things as make contributions to village development projects.

The American Chambers of Commerce abroad have continuing public relations programs to improve understanding. In its diplomatic relations our government makes an effort to put across the private enterprise story, though its effectiveness varies greatly, according to the inclinations and training of our representatives in each country. The United States government has also undertaken some major projects with this objective, such as the Commerce Department study cited above, which was designed to convince Latin Americans of the beneficial impact of American business on their economies.

Finally, individual companies and businessmen are making their own efforts both to do a better job and to convey to the public a picture of what they are doing. In the final analysis this level of effort is probably the greatest in magnitude and impact, for business is in contact with a very broad segment of the population, and its own actions are the most telling argument for or against the worth of American investment. It is important that companies *do* a good job along such lines as the Creole policies I summarized earlier and that they *tell* people what they are doing. One of the significant conclusions of a thorough study of Canadian attitudes toward American investment by the National Planning Association was that some companies, despite good performance records, have not made a favorable impression in Canada.[11] The study concluded that "the firms with good reputations were highly public relations conscious and took particular pains to publicize their good points."

Looking to the future we should therefore encourage such group efforts as the NPA pamphlet series and the BCIU programs, but our greatest hope lies in the success of business in selling its own merits.

■■■■■■■■■■ *9*

Fears of
Economic
Imperialism

"Clipping the wings of the golden goose of American enterprise without scaring the bird enough to reduce its egg production."[1]

This observation by a Canadian, Professor Harry Johnson, vividly describes one of the main problems of American business, not only in Canada but in much of the world. Other countries are anxious to benefit from American technology and capital, but they worry lest they pay too high a price in loss of control over their economic lives. So our businessmen find themselves confronted by an assortment of restricting pressures and devices which impede the flow of investment and complicate management of overseas operations.

The Yankee Octopus

The extent to which American business dominates the industries of other countries is considerable, especially among our closest neighbors. The Canadian situation has attracted most attention since the 1957 report of the Gordon Commission, a Royal Commission which surveyed the prospects of the whole Canadian economy. The Gordon Report expressed grave concern over the degree of dependence of the Canadian economy on the United States. It cited as a major factor the extent to which Canadian industry was in the hands of American management. In manufacturing, 44 percent of investment was controlled by American companies, in mining and smelting the figure was 52 percent, and in petroleum, 71 percent.

In specific industries the control was even greater. Canadian subsidiaries of Ford, General Motors, and the other American automobile companies had a virtual monopoly (95 percent) of their field; American electrical companies, including General Electric, Radio Corporation of America, and others, commanded 64 percent of that market; and Goodyear, Firestone, and other tire companies held 89 percent of the rubber products industry.[2]

For other countries we do not have a statistical picture comparable to the Gordon Report but the degree of control by American business can be readily observed. In Mexico, mining has been almost completely in the hands of a few American corporations, notably American Smelting and Refining, Anaconda, and American Metal Climax. Major segments of industry follow much the same pattern as in Canada: GM, Ford, and Chrysler have the lion's share of the automobile field; our chemical giants, such as duPont, Celanese, and Monsanto, dominate their market; Pfizer, Parke-Davis, and other American pharmaceutical firms have a major share of the drug market; and so on.

Farther away, where total American investment is smaller, the extent of American control is less. In India, for example, the only fields in which American industry has an impressive position are tire manufacturing and oil refining. Firestone and Goodyear dominate their field along with two British firms, while Standard Oil Company (N. J.) and Caltex (a subsidiary of California Standard and Texaco) have two of the three major refineries. But the national attitudes confronting American business are much the same because of the magnitude of investments by companies of other nations. The third major oil refinery is owned by the British-Dutch Shell Oil Company. Imperial Chemical Industries and other British firms have a commanding position in chemicals, German and British firms manufacture a large portion of the machinery, and so on. Thus there is the same basic concern in India over the lack of national control over industry. American companies are to some degree favored as an alternative to British investment, but the general reaction against any form of external control plays a key role in their reception.

Master in Another Man's House

Few people worry about American investments as a concerted wave of national imperialism on the part of the United States. The hundreds of companies involved are unlikely to pursue any combined course of action at the direction of the United States government to the detriment of the host nations. The concern abroad is rather that an assortment of individual company actions may add up to a pattern contrary to national interests.

Occasionally a piece of this story makes the front page in the newspapers. For example, in 1958 the Canadians were trying to improve their balance of payments position by expanding their exports to Red China. Among the products proposed were 1,000 automobiles made by Ford of Canada. But selling to Red China is contrary to United States foreign policy. So the Ford parent company, under pressure from our government, directed Ford of Canada not to make the sale. Since the other automobile makers in Canada were also American subsidiaries, the Canadian government was frustrated in carrying out what it saw as a desirable national policy. Who was right or wrong is a separate question. The important point for Canadian public opinion was that lack of control over its own industry put the country in a weak position. Eventually the deal collapsed because it appeared that the Chinese would not make the purchase, but by then the damage was done so far as Canadian public opinion was concerned.

Most of the issues are less newsworthy, but to the host country they are all important in one way or another. Many of them concern the rate of industrial development. In the extractive industries American companies have generally preferred to confine their operations in underdeveloped countries to extracting raw materials there but processing them in the United States or Europe, a policy which host nations resent. For example, drawing on an intensive research study of investment decision making, Richard Robinson describes the thinking of Firm M, which refused to construct a plant for the processing of a mineral it was mining in Chile. There would be no significant economic advantage from such a plant, and it was politically safer to bring the raw material to the United States. In addition Mr. Morgan, the president of the company, stated quite frankly: "We don't want to be at the mercy of the Chileans. So long as the minerals have to be shipped out for processing we have some leverage against the government."[3]

The importance of such leverage as a purely practical matter was illustrated in another Chilean incident in 1961. The Chilean government asked the American copper companies, Anaconda and Kennecott, to increase their production by 15 percent every three years because it wanted more export income. The companies objected because there was already ample copper production in the world and the proposed rate of expansion would probably result in a drop in prices. The government threatened to pass legislation to enforce its proposal and the companies will probably be forced to go along with the plan to some degree. In this case the companies are in a weak position because a large part of Chilean copper is processed in Chile. They know that if they buck an important government objective, the Chileans can expropriate the industry, process the copper themselves, and sell it in the world market.

In manufacturing, the issues often revolve around the extent of local manufacture. In Brazil, for example, Ford and GM resisted for some time the pressures from the government to make bodies, motors, and other components locally. For them it was far more economical to manufacture most parts in the United States and assemble them in Brazil. They ultimately gave in under the combined pressure of government directives and European competitors who, by being more amenable, were winning government favor. But the residual effect on the Brazilians was to reinforce the anti-foreign-control sentiment.

In Canada, a key issue in the manufacturing field has been the failure of American subsidiaries to develop their export business. In a fictionalized story based on real experience, Professor Gordon Huson relates the frustration of Joe McCarthy, the export manager of the Canadian subsidiary of the Goodstone Rubber Company.[4] Joe is told by his boss to increase exports and he receives letters from the Dominion government encouraging him to do so and offering various forms of help. But as a practical matter there is little he can do. All overseas Goodstone sales offices report directly to the parent company at Akron. The Canadian plant is set up to make a full range of products for Canadian sale, but its production runs are so short that almost all products can be made cheaper in Akron. Joe receives a few orders through Akron for odd-sized tires that happen to be cheaper to make in Canada or which are out of stock in Akron. But with no control over either the sales organization or the production sources, he is helpless.

The Canadian-American Committee of the National Planning Association made an extensive study of this problem and concluded that in general the Goodstone type of practice is economically sound.[5]

The committee saw little possibility for developing high-volume, low-cost production in Canada so long as tariffs restrict the flow of goods between the two countries. Many thoughtful people believe that the ultimate solution must be to break down the barriers, creating a common market so that plants in Canada will have free access to the whole American market. Neil McElroy, Chairman of the Board of Directors of Procter and Gamble and former Secretary of Defense, has made a strong plea for this solution.[6] But to the Joe McCarthys who already resent the control exercised by individual American companies like Goodstone, McElroy's ideas are as likely as not to raise images of still further subservience.

There is widespread public resistance in Canada to any suggestion of blending our two economies. The concern is partly economic, the Canadians fearing that they would be reduced to a powerless, raw-material producing adjunct to our vastly greater industrial system. But to any one reading Canadian newspapers or talking to individual Canadians, it is evident that deep-seated emotional feelings are involved. The Canadians cling desperately to their national pride and cultural identity. They are acutely conscious of the degree to which both have been chipped away and molded by the giant to the south. But they cherish dearly what independence and unique character they have preserved, and it is doubtful if they will abandon them for uncertain economic advantages.

How the Individual Feels

Beyond these broad national objectives, the resentments over American industrial control generally arise from individual frustrations, particularly of a personal and financial nature. The personal feelings are especially strong among the management men who work for American subsidiaries.

A few companies controlled from the United States are almost completely staffed by local nationals. National Cash Register Company, for example, has only 6 American citizens among its 22,000 overseas employees. But in most companies, especially in the less developed countries, a number of the top management jobs are held by Americans. According to one study of a sampling of American subsidiaries in Brazil and Mexico, 25 percent of the top-level jobs were held by Americans.[7]

During an intensive research study of local executives in subsidiaries in Mexico, I found this situation the source of strong feelings.[8] Their tenor is conveyed vividly by the remarks of Mr. Vianos, a Mexican who had been assistant sales manager of a department for five years. Three American executives had served as sales manager during that period, the third, Mr. Black, having arrived six weeks before this conversation. According to company policies, the superior job was open to local nationals, but Mr. Vianos had reached the conclusion that in practice this was not true.

> "I'm not sure if I'll stay with the company or not. There is nothing more for me here. I don't think it is fair the way things are done. I can't see any basis for sending a man down here like Mr. Black. He's sent down here with a big salary. But what is he worth? He has no contacts, he knows nothing about Mexico, he really has nothing much to contribute. It is all decided in the home office, and they don't understand the situation in the foreign units. They come down on their flying trips and talk to the top men, Mr. Pitts [the general manager], Mr. Calhoun [the assistant general manager], and Mr. Black. How can they hope to know anything about the organization? They don't understand our problems. They don't know how hard it is for the Mexicans to make ends meet. They talk about the financial problems of the men from the States, but we have ours here, too. This pension business, for example. Our people really worry about that. I'm O.K., perhaps, but for the older men this is a real worry. It used to be that a man could expect his sons to look after him when he got old. But now that's changing. Children are more independent now. They want to use their money for their own lives. A man doesn't feel good about these things."

The control from the American management cut Mr. Vianos in two ways. First, the practice of keeping Americans in the top jobs had put a ceiling on his own career. Second, it placed the determination of policies in the hands of men who, he felt, did not understand Mexican problems. In order to induce Americans to work abroad, American companies almost always pay them more than a local national would earn in the same job. And they usually receive more benefits, such as the pensions Mr. Vianos mentions. This type of situation, repeated in one form or another among several hundred executives in American-owned subsidiaries in Mexico, adds up to a substantial body of sentiment against American control — one which gathers a much broader base among sympathetic relatives, friends, and government officials.

On the financial side there are many local nationals who feel that American companies have cut them off from profiting in prime investment opportunities. This has been a key element in the Canadian debate. According to the NPA study, in only 10 percent of the American-owned subsidiaries did Canadians own more than 25 percent of the stock, and in 76 percent Canadians owned no stock at all. Prime Minister Diefenbaker in a number of speeches has emphasized his opinion: "We expect them [American-owned subsidiaries] to make available a fair portion of their equity securities for purchase by Canadians." The Gordon Commission recommended that 20 to 25 percent of the stock in American-owned subsidiaries be sold to Canadians.[9]

The strength of the desire of local investors to participate in the earnings of American companies is indicated by the good reception of many public stock issues of American companies overseas. For example, in 1956, Kaiser readily sold 63 percent of the stock in its Brazilian jeep operation and Union Carbide sold a $3.8 million public stock issue in Mexico in 1961. The supply of local money willing to invest in American companies is considerably greater than the opportunities.

The Joint Venture Movement

In country after country these assorted frustrations, resentments, and worries combine into a strong body of sentiment against American control of local business. The result is a persistent and imaginative effort to accomplish the neat trick described so aptly by Professor Johnson at the start of this chapter. American technology is in demand all over the world. Its money is welcome everywhere and desperately needed in the very underdeveloped countries which fear control the most. But the golden goose is not inclined to lay its eggs unless it can sit on them protectively until they hatch and unless it can enjoy the satisfactions of bringing its young to maturity. General Motors has little incentive simply to turn its technology and capital over to foreign companies in which it has no control.

The chief solution which has been advanced to meet this dilemma is the joint venture in which ownership is shared. In some joint ventures, the majority ownership, and thus control, remains with the American company; hence they are only a partial concession to the anti-American control sentiment. The main interest of the foreign nationals lies, therefore, in the type of joint venture in which local investors own more than 50 percent of the stock. This objective has been achieved in a number of cases. For example, Goodrich owns only 25 percent of the Goodrich tire factory in Colombia, Westinghouse owns 26 percent of Industria Electrica de Mexico, which makes its products south of the border, and American Cyanamid owns but 5 percent of Atul, an Indian company which manufactures the company's dyestuffs.

But American business has not accepted the idea on any broad scale. In 1957, joint ventures in which the American company held a minority of less than 50 percent of the ownership comprised only 5 percent of all American overseas investments. Ventures with the American firm holding more than 50 percent of the stock and the foreign investor only a minority made up another 20 percent. Previous censuses of investments did not break down the data into these two categories, but the total of all joint ventures was 17 percent of investments in 1950.[10] Thus the 1957 total of 25 percent does indicate a trend toward more joint ventures. Observations of new investments indicates, however, that the greater portion of the increase is in the minority foreign ownership category. Although many American companies are taking in some foreign capital as a concession to local sentiment, they are moving quite slowly in giving up actual control.

The tenor of American business sentiment is shown in a survey by *The International Executive* of a sample of companies which showed that 48 percent considered ventures with a minority foreign interest were "Desirable." Only 11 percent rated ventures in which they held a minority as "Desirable," while 56 percent classed them as "Acceptable if Required," and 33 percent "Not Acceptable."[11] Behind this feeling lies considerable experience which has convinced American managements that, by and large, releasing control to others is not a good idea. For example, the survey showed that 19 percent of the companies who already have joint ventures in which they own only a minority have frequent problems in administration and another 19 percent have occasional problems. Clearly many companies have quite satisfactory experiences but predicting success in advance is difficult; hence the consensus favors avoiding the risk by keeping control.

The potential disagreements which make joint ventures undesirable cover the full range of management. Many of them arise in financial and expansion policies. Sears, Roebuck withdrew from a joint venture with Walton's, an Australian firm, because Walton's wished to pay large dividends and expand slowly, whereas Sears wished to expand more rapidly by plowing back all profits into the business. This sort of disagreement is common abroad because the general tendency among foreign companies is to pay out large dividends rather than to reinvest a large portion of profits.

Other controversies may arise from differences in marketing philosophies. This story, which describes a real situation, though the names and product have been disguised, shows what can happen when a mismarriage of managements takes place.[12] John Macy, the forty-one-year-old Far Eastern Manager of the Shave-All Company, worked out an arrangement with Vishnu Rama, a prominent Indian industrialist, for the manufacture of Shave-All razors and blades in India. A new company, Shave-All of India, was set up with Shave-All holding a 10 percent interest and the Rama family the remaining 90 percent. The agreement provided that Shave-All of India had exclusive rights to Shave-All products and was obligated "to promote sales actively."

In the United States, Shave-All had been very effective with an aggressive promotion and advertising program. The company also exported razors to a number of countries, including India. Using much the same promotion methods as were used in the United States, John Macy, who was a dynamic sales manager in the best traditions of Madison Avenue, had built up sales in India rapidly. When he wrote the agreement, Macy had in mind that the Ramas would follow the same practices. Not long after the Ramas took over the management, however, he learned that sales were declining and, when he checked, he found that the marketing program had dwindled to nothing by his standards. Whereas he had had ten salesmen who actively solicited business from retailers, he found the Ramas had two men covering the whole country and doing little more than running in to stores, saying hello, dropping samples, and running out. Stocks in warehouses in key cities had been cut back so that retailers could not get new supplies quickly. Advertising had shrunk to a few unimaginative newspaper insertions. In general the whole program was a far cry from John Macy's concept of how "to promote sales actively."

But when he attempted to persuade fifty-nine-year-old Vishnu Rama that he should adopt a more aggressive approach, he met a stone wall. Rama accepted with equanimity the fact that sales had fallen, assuming that this was a normal part of the transition to local manufacture. He observed that the company was making a profit so there was no need to worry. He personally felt that advertising was unsound. Years of experience had convinced him that "a good product is its own best advertisement." Most of his competitors were English firms with long experience in India and the fact that they did no more advertising than he reinforced his views. Despite his convictions, he had authorized the newspaper ads and the giving out of samples; to him this was ample fulfillment of the agreement "to promote sales actively."

The Power Play

Because American business has not willingly accepted the idea of investing on a minority basis, the joint venture issue has evolved into something of a power struggle, a gentlemanly affair, but still a struggle. The American companies with their capital and technology would seem to hold the stronger cards in this game. But the foreign countries have a good position. Their greatest strength lies in the unwillingness of American companies to let good markets slip through their fingers. Particularly in big countries with great potentials, such as Brazil and India, they feel it is very important to maintain a market position. The alternative of accepting local investors on a joint venture basis is generally better than being refused permission to set up a factory.

If a company has a monopoly in its field, the host country cannot threaten the refusal of the permit with much force. But few companies are in that position. Most of them have important competitors, both American and foreign, and the host government can readily play one off against the other.

For example, during 1961, Company W was negotiating with the Indian government to set up a factory to make its home appliances. Knowing that the Indians wished local capital participation, the management proposed to take in a minority of 30 percent Indian capital. Meantime, however, an American competitor, Company Z, got word of Company W's negotiations. It appeared that the Indians would allow only one factory to be built for some time, so Company

Z did not want to be left out. It proposed to the Indians that it be allowed to set up a subsidiary with 45 percent Indian capital. To counter this, Company W had to accept an arrangement in which it had minority control, thus fully meeting the Indian desires.

The variations in strengths in this government-company power play have resulted in a flexible situation. The most severe restrictions are those of Japan, which will approve investments only if the American company holds 50 percent or less of the control.[13] In view of the industrial and financial development of Japan, its government is in a strong position, and it is not surprising that it has the toughest rule. Other countries tend to express a strong desire for majority control by local capital but leave the actual determination to the merits (i.e., power positions) in each case. In India, for example, there is a government resolution against majority foreign ownership, but in the past few years majority ownership has been approved for subsidiaries of Johnson & Johnson, Parke-Davis, Merck, and other American firms. Each of those named is a company whose technological capacities in the medical field give it a strong bargaining position.

A Dynamic Compromise

The outcome of the power struggle is a dynamic compromise in which both sides achieve part of their wishes but not all. As we have noted, some 5 percent of American investments abroad are on a minority basis, but in many of them practical control is retained by the American management through one device or another. For example, when duPont set up a new paint and chemical company in Mexico in 1959, an alternative proposal by another company was available to the government. As a consequence duPont had to accept an arrangement in which it would hold only 49 percent ownership. But it sold the controlling 51 percent to a Mexican bank which had no interest in factory management. Thus, at least in general operating matters, duPont has control. In this instance, however, the Mexican bank probably will exert its control on any important policy question if it differs with duPont.

More effective as a device for retaining control is the sale of the majority of the stock to the general public. Kaiser has done this in the case mentioned earlier, selling a majority of the stock in its Brazilian Willys company to 28,000 Brazilians. The 37 percent which it retained gives it full control in anything but extraordinary circumstances. Celanese, with only 48 percent of the stock of its Mexican corporation, has retained similar control by selling the balance to the general public. There are also a number of cases in which ownership is divided 50-50, but in which the American company has kept the bulk of the control by a management contract or sale of a small portion of the stock to a local national considered a reliable ally.

Most of the joint ventures, however, involve only a minority foreign participation. They do not fully meet the local national desires for control but as a practical matter they go a considerable way toward them. The fact that an opportunity to invest in the business has been given to local capital, of course, meets one main national objective. Although ultimate control rests with the American company, the presence of local capital and usually one or more local nationals on the board of directors means that the national viewpoint is constantly represented. The feelings of executives, such as Mr. Vianos, that the American management does not understand the problems of the local personnel are likely to be reduced and their career opportunities may be enhanced if they have a fellow countryman on the board to speak for them. Thus, although minority foreign participation is not what the local nationals really want, it takes the curse off American investment, making it considerably more palatable.

Despite the growth of joint ventures, 75 percent of our investments are in the 95 percent or more American ownership class, which means that local capital at best plays a purely nominal part in management. Still even in this large segment of our overseas operations, the sentiment against American control has had a marked effect. Conscious of the possibility that changes might be forced upon them, American companies have made serious efforts to bend their practices to meet the wishes of the nations in which they are operating. For example, when the Mexican government expressed a desire in the mid-fifties to see local manufacturing of automobile components accelerated, Ford, GM, and the other big companies quickly endorsed the plan. They had had enough experience by then with the difficulties of adjusting to accelerated manufacturing plans dictated by the Argentine and Brazilian governments so that they saw the wisdom of cooperating in a voluntary program. A committee was set up composed of government officials, purchasing directors of the automobile companies, and executives representing suppliers. This group carefully reviewed the possibilities and problems of producing one product after another, deciding that some should be made now, some a little later, some by a Mexican company with help from an American supplier, some by one of the automobile companies, and so on. The whole scheme moved along with an agreeable acceptance by the companies that when something is inevitable they might as well relax and enjoy it.

There has been similar steady progress in the advancement of local nationals to higher responsibilities. The pace is slow, but one by one men move ahead. Indeed, despite the forebodings of Mr. Vianos, when Mr. Calhoun, the assistant general manager, was transferred shortly after our conversation, a Mexican took over his job and the company was quite serious about its desires to go still further.

An Uncertain Future

How the worries about American control will be resolved is as yet quite uncertain. Much probably depends upon what the American companies themselves do. There are those that feel that as the underdeveloped countries get their economies rolling and the need for American capital and technology becomes less, the power balance will turn against American business and it will be forced increasingly to enter into joint ventures as a minority partner. On the other hand, it is true that in the most developed area — the European countries — the pressures on American business to share control are the lightest. It is also clear that American companies are very anxious to avoid giving up control. Under the continuing pressure from foreign governments, it seems most likely, therefore, that they will keep working toward accommodating the national desires for industrial progress, personal opportunities, and financial benefits by adjusting their own policies but in most instances without surrendering control.

■■■■■■■■■■■■ *10*

Carrots
and
Umbrellas

Are American overseas investments growing fast enough?

By normal business standards, the answer to this question is an emphatic yes. While there have been specific failures, American industry, by and large, has acted with vigor and skill to capitalize on its opportunities abroad. Overseas investments have grown rapidly and American firms are earning good profits from them.

But, from the point of view of United States foreign policy, the results have been much less satisfactory. American investments have not flowed strongly into the places where their contributions were needed most to foster economic development. In the Cold War struggle, top priority is assigned to building the economies of the underdeveloped sections of the world and building them on a base of democracy and free enterprise. Yet the rate of new investment in these areas, especially in the vital field of manufacturing, has been distressingly low. To meet this shortcoming, a variety of proposals have been advanced to entice American business into the less developed countries.

The Economic Backwaters

Since World War II, American overseas investments have quadrupled, rising from $8 billion in 1945 to $33 billion at the end of 1960. This tremendous expansion, steered by the dictates of the profit motive, has been concentrated in the fields which offered the greatest business opportunities, as shown in Figure 25. A third of our investments are in Canada, whose proximity and characteristics make it a natural area of expansion. There is virtually no political risk, the economy is strong, and the people are so similar to ours that little adaptation to the environment is required. With ample incentive and few deterrents, American companies of all sorts and sizes have moved into Canada in force. As we saw in Chapter 9, this movement has aroused some Canadian ire, but economically it has made an important contribution to Canadian growth.

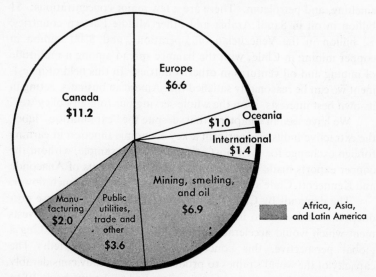

FIG. 25. Distribution of United States direct investments abroad at end of 1960 (in billions of dollars).
Source: Appendix, Table 4.

A fifth of the investments are in Europe, and they have had the greatest growth in recent years. Of the $2.9 billion total increase in overseas investments from 1959 to 1960, $1.3 billion, or about 45 percent, was in Europe. The investments in Europe certainly serve our foreign policy interests in that they strengthen the economies of a major sector of the free world. But we no longer worry about Europe as we did in the immediate postwar years, and it is likely that the European economic boom would continue even without as much new American investment. Another billion dollars of investment is in Oceania, mostly in Australia, which is also a relatively developed area. And $1.4 billion listed as "International" is in shipping, operating chiefly out of Liberia and Panama. In all, $20 billion, about 60 percent of our investments, are in economically advanced countries. These investments are valuable to us because, as we noted in Chapter 1, they permit us to participate in the economic growth of these regions, but they are not an important factor in the Cold War struggle in the less developed areas.

Of the 40 percent of our investments which are in the under-developed areas, $7 billion, or a little more than half, are in mining, smelting, and petroleum. There are a few major concentrations: $1 billion in oil in Saudi Arabia and other Middle Eastern countries, $2 billion in the Venezuelan oil operations, and $500 million in copper mining in Chile, with the balance spread among a multitude of mining and oil ventures in other countries. In this field of investment we can be reasonably satisfied that American business, acting in its own best interests, is on the whole serving our foreign policy well.

We have seen in Chapter 8 that, despite the "exploitation" label, the extractive industries perform a key economic function in earning foreign exchange for their host countries. For example, without the copper exports made possible by the huge investments of Anaconda and Kennecott, Chile's economic development would be much slower.

The demands by Chile that the copper companies increase production would seem to imply that there is room for further investment which would accelerate economic development. But taking a global perspective, this conclusion cannot be supported. The capacity of the world's mines to produce copper already considerably exceeds demand, so that production has had to be cut back 10 to 15 percent in recent years by the major producers. And the same problem of overcapacity is found in oil, lead, zinc, and virtually every mineral industry. Thus there is little possibility of further increasing production, and acceleration of investment in the extractive field is not justified.

American business has demonstrated its willingness to invest heavily in mines and oil wells to meet its raw-material needs, even under relatively adverse conditions. Currently, for example, the Olin Mathieson Corporation is developing a new aluminum operation in Guinea despite the risks of communist infiltration in that country, and several American oil companies have persisted in oil exploration in North Africa, where the political future is highly uncertain. It appears that the pressures to meet raw-material needs and find profitable outlets for investment are sufficient in themselves so that American business can be expected on the whole to do the job in this field. Government help will doubtless be welcome, but we can regard private investment in extractive operations as a generally strong phase in our program to foster economic development.

The weak spot is in the manufacturing operations in less developed countries which, along with public utilities and trading, agricultural, and banking activities, make up the remainder of our investments. Industrial development is the heart of the economic progress for these countries. They must be able to make the things their people need for a better way of life: shoes, bicycles, automobiles, and a myriad of other products. To do this they must have factories. Since we want to see the private enterprise system flourish, we look to local and imported capital to build the factories.

The $2 billion invested in manufacturing in Latin America, Asia, and Africa is a useful contribution in this direction. We saw in Chapter 8 that American manufacturing activities in Latin America are playing a vital role in the economic growth of the region. But viewed against the job to be done, the rate of new investment is discouraging, particularly in the critical areas where rapid growth is most urgently needed.

The greater part of the new investments is going into countries whose industrialization is furthest advanced. For example, American investments in Brazilian manufacturing jumped from $438 million in 1959 to $515 in 1960, an increase of 17 percent, while those in Chile rose only from $21 million to $22 million, a mere 5 percent increase from a total which is much smaller even in proportion to the relative sizes of the countries (population of Brazil, 68 million; of Chile, 7 million). Similarly, manufacturing investments in Japan rose from $71 million to $91 million in this period, while those in India increased only from $43 million to $51 million.

This pattern of manufacturing investment is the result of sound management thinking. We can see its logic in the recent experience of International Harvester, a company with a long and successful career in overseas operations. About 30 percent of IH sales are made by overseas units, and the company has expanded abroad wherever it felt it saw a reasonable chance of earning a fair profit. About two thirds of the company's investments are currently in factories in Canada, Europe, and Oceania. The Canadian and European subsidiaries have been the main focus of interest in recent years because they are the ones showing the strongest sales increases.

There are two IH factories in Latin America, one in Brazil, and one in Mexico. These subsidiaries are doing fairly well and there has been some new investment, for example, an expansion of truck production capacity in Brazil. But Latin-American sales have been discouraging, dropping about 10 percent in 1960. There is an assembly plant in the Philippines, but this is a special case because it dates from the period of United States control in that area. Otherwise, there are no factories in the less developed countries. International Harvester sells almost everywhere but serves most of the Asian, African, and Latin-American markets with exports from its plants in developed countries.

This story is especially significant, of course, because IH products, tractors and agricultural equipment, are just the type of thing which every underdeveloped country would like to make itself. International Harvester is under constant pressure from one country or another to undertake new manufacturing ventures. The problem is that the company simply cannot justify most of these proposals on economic grounds because the potential markets are too small and the risks are too great.

Turkey provides a typical case in point. In the early 1950's, Turkey asked International Harvester to start manufacturing tractors.[1] At the time there were only about 40,000 tractors in the country. Sales of all companies had been running around 3,000 per year, but American financial aid had been forcing the pace, so the company had to expect a somewhat lower level of sales as normal. A great variety of sizes of track-laying and wheeled tractors were sold. Thus at best the company could contemplate production runs in the low hundreds for a single type of tractor, resulting in costs well above those in a large plant in Europe. To this basic economic problem had to be added the difficulties of obtaining parts and skilled labor in the undeveloped Turkish economy and the political risks of an immature democracy constantly threatened by Russia. All told, the proposition was not sound.

The company was under the type of pressure we discussed in Chapter 1: the threat of possible exclusion if another company started manufacturing. In fact, in 1954 Minneapolis-Moline did agree to set up a tractor factory. However, the reality of the deterrents considered by International Harvester has been confirmed by the very slow progress of this new plant.[2]

This story with very few variations could be repeated for company after company in country after country. It spells out the practical management decisions which add up to the statistics we have seen. In virtually every underdeveloped country one finds a few American companies which have gone into manufacturing. In Turkey, for example, there is a General Electric light bulb factory, Squibb makes pharmaceutical products, and there are a handful of other American plants. But the rate of new investment is painfully slow in the face of the pressing need for rapid increases in standards of living to stem the tide of communism.

Giving a Helping Hand

Government officials and business leaders alike are acutely conscious of this dilemma, and earnest efforts have been made to resolve it. Clearly there is the alternative of channeling aid funds into government-owned factories abroad. But few people favor that solution. It does not foster private enterprise, and government factories are not generally efficient and progressive in management. The urgent need, therefore, is to find ways to bring more private business into less developed countries.

There have been a few quite radical proposals to meet the problem. In 1961, Senator Jacob Javits introduced a bill in Congress to establish a Peace by Investment Corporation. The corporation would be set up initially with $100 million of government money but the ultimate intent is to draw on private capital to the extent of $2 billion to maintain the project on an independent basis. It would provide a vehicle for channeling United States capital into useful private ventures in underdeveloped countries.[3] Another scheme has been proposed by Donald K. David of the Committee for Economic Development under which the United States government would finance factories abroad and contract for their management with private firms.[4] Under his plan our government might have paid for the construction of a tractor factory in Turkey and then signed a management contract with International Harvester. The United States government would then be carrying the business and political risks, but the plant would have the benefits of an experienced management. Such schemes have attracted little support, however, because the American public has not accepted the need for such major steps and because they pose a variety of administrative hazards. For example, Mr. David's proposal would involve decisions as to which company would be chosen to manage each plant and what fees would be paid — decisions replete with hazards of favoritism, political logrolling, and the like.

Thus most interest has focused on devices which would raise the profit potentials or reduce the risks in individual management decisions. The logical assumption is that as the economics-risks equation in each manufacturing proposal changes, there must come a point where it will be sufficiently favorable so that the company will be willing to make the investment. If International Harvester could have seen a greater economic return from a tractor factory in Turkey or if the risks from a political upheaval or from the Russians were reduced, it might have gone ahead with setting up a plant.

Economic Carrots

On the economic side, the main efforts have been made by foreign governments which have provided a variety of incentives for foreign investors. In some cases they have made loans of local currency to finance part of a new plant or have built a factory and leased it on very favorable terms to the foreign investor. The Minneapolis-Moline tractor factory in Turkey was set up in much this manner. A Turkish agricultural agency put up $5 million to cover the cost of the building and initial operations. The American company had only to invest $2 million, covering machinery, technicians, and other costs for which United States dollars were needed.

But, as the financial resources of these countries are limited, the chief aids they have been able to provide have been market protection and tax relief. Pakistan is a good example of a country which has tried very hard to attract investment with these two devices as the chief carrots. A new firm in Pakistan which meets certain criteria does not have to pay taxes for as long as six years and the government will not allow competing products to be imported if the new firm's prices are no more than 15 percent above the cost of the imports.

Unfortunately these efforts by foreign governments are frustrated in part by the United States government. The benefits of tax concessions made by the host government are completely lost when dividends are paid to the American parent under current laws. If the Maxon Tool Company sets up a plant in Pakistan, for instance, it may receive an exemption from the 45 percent Pakistani income tax for six years and thus keep its full profits so long as it does not pay dividends. But when it does pay a dividend, the parent company has to pay the full 52 percent United States tax on the dividend. If

Maxon had been paying the 45 percent Pakistani income tax, the parent company would have received a credit from the United States government for that tax, thus greatly reducing the United States tax. So Maxon ends up paying virtually the same amount of tax whether it has the exemption or not.

The ironic part of this story is that Pakistan's effort to give Maxon a break is not only frustrated, but the Pakistanis end by letting the United States government collect a large sum of taxes which they gave up. In view of the efforts of the United States to shore up the finances of less developed countries, this borders on the ridiculous.

In fact, tax exemption programs in Pakistan and other countries have not been rendered fully ineffective by United States taxation but only because of precisely the tax deferral devices which the U.S. Treasury is attacking. By the skillful use of the tax-haven companies we observed in Chapter 4, American investors are able to hold these earnings outside the United States and make the most of the tax benefits. Maxon, for example, would set up the Pakistani operation as a subsidiary of a Swiss tax-haven company. It would expect for several years to plow back its earnings into expansion in Pakistan. Then, when the Pakistani operation matured, it could pay dividends to the Swiss company, which could then put the money into a new operation in another country.

The Treasury proposals to tax the profits of tax-haven companies would, of course, make this system impossible. But, even without this added hazard, the present state of affairs is highly undesirable. We should be helping rather than complicating the efforts of other countries. Most of our government tax experts are unhappy with this situation and efforts have been made to correct it.

The chief corrective device is the concept of "tax sparing." The idea of tax sparing as first officially proposed by Secretary of Treasury George Humphrey in 1954 amounts to "giving credit for general foreign income taxes which are waived for an initial limited period as we now grant credit for taxes which are imposed."[5] For the Maxon Tool Company it would mean that when the Pakistani subsidiary paid a dividend to the parent company, the United States government would treat it as though the 45 percent Pakistani income tax had been paid. Maxon would receive a large credit, virtually offsetting the 52 percent United States tax and thus would receive the full benefit of the Pakistani exemption.

There are objections to this proposal, notably that it is subject to abuse. If Congress were to pass a law providing for universal tax sparing, a variety of schemes might be concocted to take advantage of it. For example, the government of Latinia, perhaps with the encouragement of American firms, could enact a special tax applicable only to foreign investors, bringing its total income tax up to 52 percent and then grant wholesale exemptions. The American companies could claim a credit for payment of the 52 percent income tax, which would offset the whole United States tax. It isn't pleasant to think that such things could be done, but as a practical matter Treasury officials know they can and are justifiably cautious.

To avoid such shenanigans the Treasury has advocated adoption of tax-sparing provisions applicable to specific foreign laws. For some time our government has been negotiating with other countries tax treaties covering various areas in which we have overlapping taxes. The government proposes to incorporate the tax-sparing provision into these treaties where it is appropriate. In 1957 a treaty was signed with Pakistan including the tax-sparing clause. The Senate, however, has never approved the treaty, and the tax-sparing idea has made no further progress.

This is a very unfortunate state of affairs which is everyone's fault and no one's fault. The problem is that there is no one who counts in a political sense who really cares much about tax sparing. Companies with overseas operations favor it, but it does not loom large in their affairs. It affects only a small portion of their business and, given the use of tax-haven companies, its value lies in the fairly distant future. They have therefore devoted their time and energy to larger and more immediate tax questions, such as the Boggs bill and the tax-haven issue. Our Treasury and the foreign-aid people are also interested, but they too have bigger battles to fight in Congress. Those who have most to gain are the foreign governments, but they have no votes in the United States and thus attract little attention in Congress. The tax-sparing idea is not dead, but it will probably never be put over until someone throws real weight behind it. In the meantime, this problem adds one more argument to the already strong case against attempting to tax the tax-haven companies.

A Protective Umbrella

By economic inducements, underdeveloped countries have been able to make new investments look invitingly profitable. But the menacing bogy of loss through expropriation or some other calamity has still hovered over them, scaring away potential investors. Pakistan might arrange tax and other factors so that the Maxon Tool Company could make, let us say, a 30 percent profit per year on its investment. But the short history of Pakistan has included some violent political upheavals and periods of severe economic stress. Thus, even though conditions at the moment seem favorable, Maxon would have to consider the possibility of major difficulties. If a revolutionary government nationalized its plant, the whole investment might well be lost. A 30 percent profit looks large by itself, but against such a risk it doesn't measure up well.

To overcome this major block to new investments the United States government has developed an investment guarantee system under which a company can insure its operations against major risks. Maxon, for example, could arrange a guarantee for its investment in Pakistan. Then, if the plant were expropriated, it would be assured compensation for the loss from the United States government.

The investment guarantee program started in 1948 under the Marshall Plan. At that time, our major effort was directed to building up Europe and saving it from communism. Many American companies were leery of investing because the threats of Russian aggression or internal communist take-over were very real in many countries. In addition the European countries were so weak financially that companies were concerned about their ability to obtain dollars to bring profits home.

So the guarantee program was conceived as a government-sponsored insurance system. For a modest fee a company received protection against the major investment risks: war, expropriation, and inability to obtain dollars to repay capital and to pay interest or dividends. For example, in 1949 the Singer Manufacturing Company wanted to lend $800,000 to its French subsidiary to finance new production equipment for its sewing machine factory. The French situation was very shaky at the time; hence Singer obtained a guarantee from the United States government. It paid a fee of 1 percent per year and in return was assured that dollar exchange would be available to repay part of the loan each year, together with the interest.

With the full recovery of Europe, the guarantee program there has terminated. But the idea is considered sound and its application has been steadily broadened for the underdeveloped areas. By the end of 1961, a company could obtain a guarantee for investments in any one of forty-five countries. Each of these countries has signed an agreement with our government giving certain assurances for the protection of the investments. The agreements also provide for approval of each guaranteed investment by the foreign government. Thus, the Singer loan was not guaranteed until the French had agreed that the expansion of the sewing machine factory was economically good for France. In this manner, our government avoids underwriting ventures which are not in the interests of sound economic development abroad.

For the first decade of its operation, the guarantee program was not extensively used. Up to 1959, 244 individual guarantees had been made, covering only about $300 million, or 2 percent of the $15 billion of new investments in that period. Recently, more companies have been using the system. By March, 1961, the number of guarantees had risen to 428, totaling $571 million. In addition, applications for $2.6 billion were in the hands of the United States government awaiting either completion of company investment plans or the signing of agreements with countries not yet in the guarantee system.

The increase in interest in the guarantees is due to their extension to the less developed countries. So long as the program was largely confined to Europe it served no major need. A few companies, such as Singer, felt the added protection was worth while. But the recovery of Europe was relatively strong and rapid and most companies felt that the guarantees were not worth the trouble and expense.

For investment in the less developed countries, however, the risks are considerable. While, as we have noted, there is still too little investment going into these countries, the number of new American plants being set up in them has increased, causing greater interest in guarantees.

Reinforcing this increase in interest have been recent world developments, especially Castro's Cuban revolution. American investments in Cuba before the revolution added up to almost $1 billion. Virtually all of this property has been expropriated and the companies are unlikely to recover any significant portion of it from the Castro regime, which is financially weak. Some companies have suffered severe losses. Texaco, for example, has lost an oil refinery worth $50 million. This experience has driven home to businessmen the very real risks of serious trouble, even in nearby countries.

With increasing interest in it, the guarantee program was further strengthened in the 1961 foreign-aid bill. A company can now obtain insurance against risks of insurrection and revolution as well as those previously covered. And the government is working to widen the area covered by signing agreements with additional countries.

How effective this program will be in stimulating more investments in the less developed countries is uncertain. As Castroism has gained momentum throughout Latin America, there has been a notable cooling of interest in new investments there. It is quite clear that no company wants to throw its assets into a fire even if it knows the insurance company will pay for the loss. A company can never recover all of the lost effort of setting up a plant, and the initial trouble is not worth while without a real prospect of profit. So the guarantees can at best only tip the balance a little in every decision, reducing somewhat the risks and making some investments possible which would not otherwise take place. Despite these limited prospects, however, the guarantee program is one of the few definite contributions which the United States government can make to encourage private investment, and its continuation and expansion is therefore sound policy.

The Investment Climate

Tax sparing and investment guarantees are two specific devices for increasing investment in underdeveloped countries. They are useful but not nearly so important as the combination of conditions which come under the heading of "the investment climate" in each country. To visualize the meaning of "the investment climate" we can best look inside the mind of John Maddox, the president of a company, as he considers two countries, Germany and India, as possible places to invest.

In Germany, Mr. Maddox sees that private enterprise is thoroughly endorsed by the government, the political situation stable, and the financial condition of the country strong. He can set up a plant with confidence that the government will respect his right to operate with the freedom he is used to in the United States. Not only is there little risk of expropriation but he will not be bothered with an undue amount of meddling and interference by government economic planners and minor officials. Mr. Maddox feels comfortable about the prospect. The investment climate is good.

In India, though, Mr. Maddox gets quite a different impression.

The political situation is relatively stable but the outlook for freedom of operation is not promising. Prime Minister Nehru has declared that India believes in a "socialistic pattern of society." Exactly what this means is not too clear. There are official assurances that most manufacturing will be left to private enterprise, but the government owns plants making a variety of products: steel, drugs and so on. The border line between the private and public spheres of operation seems to be flexible. Moreover, even in the "private" area, business is subject to much government regulation. For example, Mr. Maddox learns that in 1955 a government commission made a detailed study of the financial accounts of Firestone and the other tire companies. It recomputed their costs in ways which the companies regarded as unfair and then, after determining what it thought was a proper profit level, established new prices for tires. In addition it made very critical comments about the advertising and selling practices of the companies, implying that, if they were not changed, still further interference might be expected. Out of this and other stories Mr. Maddox builds up a picture of the investment climate in India which, by his standards, is quite unfavorable.

These impressions are of vital importance in the problem of stimulating new investments in less developed countries. Investment decisions are made by individuals like Mr. Maddox, men with feelings, men who worry about their jobs and their profits. Mr. Maddox may want to see India progress, but he is not anxious to set up a business where the investment climate is uncomfortable.

Improving the investment climate in a country like India is a difficult task. The Indians have firm convictions about the soundness of their ways. They think that strict economic planning and supervision of business are essential to their economic development. Many of them are basically inclined to socialism and rather suspicious of businessmen. They want men like Mr. Maddox to invest money in their country, but they are not willing to change their ways much for the sake of such investments. In view of the immensity of their development task and the small contribution American private investment has made to it thus far, the Indians' heavy reliance on government direction is certainly understandable.

There is not a great deal the United States government can do about the investment climate. Still it is such a large factor in management decisions that it has to be given attention, and our government is officially committed to doing what it can to improve the investment climate abroad. Our effectiveness in this direction varies greatly from country to country, however, and there is ample room for improvement. In particular, it is important that we send men abroad who are sympathetic to the concepts of private enterprise and have the will and ability to improve the investment climate.

An Uphill Struggle

This chapter cannot end on an optimistic note because the prospects are not encouraging. But it must end with an exhortation to imaginative and determined action because the urgency for achievement is great.

There is a steady flow of new investment into manufacturing in the less developed countries. At times, it seems to be gaining momentum under favorable influences. Since about 1958, for example, India has shown a greater willingness to accommodate its policies to the feelings of private enterprises, and the rate of new investment has picked up. Similarly, the investment guarantee program has broadened to provide needed protection in many marginal situations.

But every time we seem to be making progress, something happens to set back the whole process. The latest blow was Castro. His nationalizations have put a damper on hundreds of business plans. When he seized the Texaco refinery in Cuba, proposals for new investments in every Latin-American republic were slowed down or killed. It will take many years to restore in American businessmen the confidence destroyed by that act.

Looking to the future, we must redouble our efforts to expand the manufacturing activities of our private enterprises in under-developed countries. Their contributions are, of course, valuable to the growth of physical production. But more important in the struggle to preserve free democratic institutions throughout the world, private enterprise is a vital force. The choice of the under-developed countries is clear. They are determined to expand their production. If private enterprise does not do the job, they will increasingly resort to government-managed production. That in itself is detrimental to private institutions and it opens the door to communism. Castro-like setbacks are probably inevitable as part of the continuing Cold War and the animosity toward capitalism and colonialism around the world. We must not allow such setbacks to scare us off, for that would be tantamount to admitting defeat in an important phase of the Cold War. Rather, they must stir us on to determined and imaginative efforts to expand the contributions of private enterprise in crucial areas. If our investment guarantees and other devices are not enough, then we must seek out new approaches which will throw the full force of American business into the fray.

A
Look
Ahead

International business is highly beneficial to the United States. Through exports and overseas investments we are able to participate in the economic expansion of other nations. Imports bring to our shores essential foods and raw materials as well as manufactured goods which other countries can make more economically than we. But these benefits cannot be fully realized unless we are adept in handling the difficult problems of adjusting our own industry to increased imports, keep our international payments in balance, and make our overseas operations acceptable to host nations. In the past we have repeatedly fallen into difficulties in our international business through failure to foresee the nature of these problems and to meet them realistically and constructively as they arose.

It is well worth our while, therefore, to look ahead at this point to see what sort of problems we can expect in the next decade and what we must do to resolve them in the best interests of our country. It seems certain that the economies of the world will make great forward strides in the next ten years. Major increases are being forecast in the gross national products of all areas: 71 percent for Japan, 73 percent for Canada and Mexico, 63 percent for South America, 55 percent for Western Europe, and 42 percent for the United States.[1] Although these figures are certainly crude guesses, rates of growth of comparable magnitude are currently being experienced by these areas and there is every reason to assume they will continue. This growth will cause an expansion and diversification of demand for the tremendous range of products which American

165

industry can provide. At the same time, the expansion of the American economy and the drain on our domestic raw-material resources will create ever-greater demand for imported goods.

Specifically we may expect these developments affecting our international business. First, as standards of living rise abroad, markets for consumer goods will continue to broaden. The trend toward overseas production observed in Chapter 1 will continue, with foreign manufacture displacing United States exportation of more products in still more countries.

Second, the parallel expansion of American exports of specialized products observed in Chapters 1 and 2 will also continue pushing our total exports ever higher.

Third, we should be able to increase our exports of agricultural commodities. One of the tragic inequities of our current world economic situation is the maldistribution of food supplies. The United States has a major problem of excess agricultural output. Other nations, such as India and Pakistan, are struggling to produce enough to keep their populations fed at a bare subsistence level. We may hope that as one of the consequences of economic progress these underfed nations will be able to produce enough so that they can export more manufactured goods and be able in turn to buy more of our agricultural excesses.

Fourth, on the import side we will clearly have increased our purchases of raw materials, but, more important, it will be economically sound to import a greater volume and variety of manufactured products. With the earnings from our expanded exports of specialized industrial products and agricultural commodities, we will be able to benefit from the low costs which foreign mass production of consumer items will permit.

One can readily visualize the outcome of these trends. By the 1970's American companies will have overseas factories with double or more their present productive capacity. Exports of mass-consumption items will have dwindled to a low level. At the same time, exports of machinery, specialized chemicals, and similar products will have increased and the expanded outflow of grains, cotton, and other farm produce will be drawing off the productive surpluses of our land. We will, in turn, be importing vastly greater quantities of petroleum and minerals, and imports of basic consumer goods, from textiles to electrical appliances to simpler mechanical products, will have taken over a greater share of the American market.

What does all this require of us? Clearly the heart of the whole process is change, and the key to success must be flexibility — the ability to foster and benefit from changes, not to resist and suffer from their effects. We must be ready and able to expand our investments abroad to keep pace with the rate of expansion in each country. We must give continuing attention to the problems of overcoming the fears of exploitation and American control among the people of other nations. We must be alert to the new export opportunities which will open up for specialized products and agricultural goods at the same time that our exports of mass-produced manufactured products decline. Finally, we must leave the door open to the expansion of imports of manufactured goods, giving thoughtful attention to the problems of adjustment of industries which are hurt by competition from imports.

If we demonstrate wisdom and flexibility in our business and government policies in dealing with these changes as they come along, then as a nation we will be able to reap the great rewards which international business proffers us.

■■■■■■■■■■■

References

Chapter 1

1. U.S. Department of Commerce, *U.S. Business Investments in Foreign Countries* (Washington, D.C.: Government Printing Office, 1960), p. 35, and *Survey of Current Business*, September, 1961, p. 23.
2. E. R. Barlow and Ira T. Wender, *Foreign Investment and Taxation* (Englewood Cliffs, N.J.: Prentice-Hall, Inc., 1955), p. 432.
3. H. J. Heinz, "Why Abroad?" *Planning Overseas Operations* (New York: International Management Association, 1956), p. 6.
4. *Business Week*, September 9, 1961, p. 61.

Chapter 2

1. For a fuller discussion of this subject see *Industrial Development Abroad — Threat or Opportunity?* (Washington, D.C.: Committee for a National Trade Policy, 1959).
2. Emile Benoit, *Europe at Sixes and Sevens* (New York: Columbia University Press, 1961), pp. 145–165.
3. Frederick H. Harbison, *et al.*, *Steel Management on Two Continents* (Chicago: The Industrial Relations Center, 1955).
4. John Fayerweather, *Management of International Operations* (New York: McGraw-Hill Book Company, 1960), pp. 388–397.
5. Benoit, *op. cit.*, p. 174.
6. *Ibid.*, pp. 175–181.

Chapter 3

1. Beatrice N. Vaccara, *Employment and Output in Protected Industries* (Washington, D.C.: The Brookings Institution, 1960), pp. 88–97.
2. Laurence A. Knapp, "The Buy American Act: A Review and Assessment," *Columbia Law Review*, March, 1961, pp. 435, 448.
3. Oscar R. Strackbein, *Causes of Unemployment in the Coal and Other Domestic Industries.* Hearings before the Senate Committee on Labor and Public Welfare, 84th Cong., 1st Sess. (1955), p. 194.
4. Walter S. Salant, "Employment Effects of United States Import Liberalization," *American Economic Review*, May, 1960, p. 425.
5. M. E. Kreinin, "Effect of Tariff Changes on Imports," *American Economic Review*, June, 1961, p. 321.
6. Howard S. Piquet, *Aid, Trade and the Tariff* (New York: Thomas Y. Crowell Company, 1953), p. 23.
7. National Planning Association, *Local Impact of Foreign Trade* (Washington, D.C.: 1960), p. 34.
8. Percy W. Bidwell, *What the Tariff Means to American Industries* (New York: Harper & Brothers, 1956), p. 283.
9. Franz Gehrels, "Freer Trade and the Payments Problem," *Business Horizons*, Spring, 1961, p. 73.
10. Irving B. Kraviz, "Wages and Foreign Trade," *Review of Economics and Statistics*, February, 1956, pp. 14–30.
11. Harry G. Johnson, "The Case for Tariff Reform," *Business Quarterly*, Spring, 1961, p. 32.
12. John Lindeman and Walter S. Salant, *Assistance for Adjustment to Tariff Reductions* (Washington, D.C.: The Brookings Institution, 1960).
13. Commission on Foreign Economic Policy, *Report to the President and the Congress*, January, 1954 (Washington, D.C.: Superintendent of Documents), pp. 55–58.
14. Horace B. McCoy, "United States Foreign Economic Policy," *Vital Speeches of the Day*, May 1, 1961, p. 429.

Chapter 4

1. The credit allowed is equal to

$$\frac{\text{Foreign Taxes paid} \times \text{Dividends from Subsidiary}}{\text{Subsidiary Profits before Foreign Taxes}}$$

Thus the tax on the profits and dividends from a subsidiary in a country with a 30% tax rate would be:

Subsidiary profits	$100.00	
Foreign tax	30.00	30.00
Net paid as dividend to parent	70.00	
U.S. tax @ 52%	36.40	
Credit: $\dfrac{30 \times 70}{100}$	21.00	
Net U.S. tax due	15.40	15.40
Total Taxes Paid		$45.40

This system results in payment of less than 52 percent total foreign and United States tax when the foreign tax is below 52 percent. It has been subject to considerable criticism and the Kennedy administration has proposed substituting a "grossing-up" system that would set the United States tax at the difference between 52 percent and the foreign tax, thus giving total tax payments of 52 percent.

2. Enid Baird Lovell, *Organizing Foreign-Base Corporations* (New York: National Industrial Conference Board, 1961), pp. 7–9.
3. U.S. House of Representatives, Committee on Ways and Means, *President's 1961 Tax Recommendations*, Washington, D.C.: Government Printing Office, vol. 1, 1961, p. 30.
4. *Ibid.*, p. 32.
5. *Ibid.*, p. 29.
6. *Ibid.*, p. 33.

Chapter 5

1. *The International Position of the Dollar* (New York: Committee for Economic Development, 1961), p. 56.
2. "And Industry Gives Its Views," *International Executive*, Spring, 1961, p. 33.
3. U.S. House of Representatives, Committee on Ways and Means, *President's 1961 Tax Recommendations* (Washington, D.C.: Government Printing Office, 1961), p. 31.

Chapter 6

1. "The West Is Risking a Credit Collapse," *Fortune*, July, 1961, p. 127.

Chapter 7

1. U.S. Senate, Committee on Foreign Relations, *U.S.–U.S.S.R. Trade Relations* (Washington, D.C.: Government Printing Office, 1959), p. 15.
2. Business International, *The Communist World as Customer & Competitor* (New York: Haynes Publishing Company, 1959), p. 9.
3. U.S. Senate, Committee on Foreign Relations, *op. cit.*, p. 4.
4. Cleveland Lane, "The U.S. Chemical Industry's Views on Trade with the Soviets," in *Aspects of East-West Trade* (New York: American Management Association, 1960), pp. 60–67.
5. J. B. Scott, "The Anglo-Soviet Five-Year Trade Agreement," in *Aspects of East-West Trade*, p. 28.
6. *Ibid.*
7. Joint Economic Committee, *A New Look at Trade Policy toward the Communist Bloc* (Washington, D.C.: Government Printing Office, 1961), p. 35.
8. Joseph S. Berliner, *Soviet Economic Aid* (New York: Frederick A. Praeger, Inc., 1958), p. 151.

Chapter 8

1. Wendell C. Gordon, *The Expropriation of Foreign-Owned Property in Mexico* (Washington, D.C.: American Council on Public Affairs, 1941), p. 81.
2. Stacy May and Galo Plaza, *The United Fruit Company in Latin America* (Washington, D.C.: National Planning Association, 1958), p. 112.
3. Gordon, *op. cit.*, p. 112.
4. Marvin Bernstein, "History and Economic Organization of the Mexican Mining Industry, 1890–1940" (Unpublished doctoral thesis; Austin: Institute of Latin American Studies, University of Texas), pp. 575–577.
5. Vernon H. Jensen, *Heritage of Conflict, Labor Relations in the Non-Ferrous Mining Industry Up to 1930* (Ithaca, N.Y.: Cornell University Press, 1950).
6. Wayne C. Taylor and John Lindeman, *The Creole Petroleum Corporation in Venezuela* (Washington, D.C.: National Planning Association, 1955).
7. Fayerweather, *op. cit.*, pp. 222–232.

8. *Ibid.*, pp. 541–547.
9. U.S. Department of Commerce, *U.S. Investments in the Latin American Economy* (Washington, D.C.: Government Printing Office, 1957).
10. Raymond W. Miller, *Can Capitalism Compete?* (New York: The Ronald Press Company, 1959), pp. 63–64.
11. John Lindeman and John Armstrong, *Policies and Practices of United States Subsidiaries in Canada* (Washington, D.C.: National Planning Association, 1961), p. 79.

Chapter 9

1. Harry G. Johnson, "The Case for Tariff Reform," *Business Quarterly*, Spring, 1961, p. 28.
2. Lindeman and Armstrong, *op. cit.*, p. 17.
3. Richard D. Robinson, "Conflicting Interests in International Business Investment," *Boston University Business Review*, Spring, 1960.
4. Gordon Huson, "The Goodstone Rubber Corporation of Canada," in Fayerweather, *op. cit.*, pp. 547–554.
5. Lindeman and Armstrong, *op. cit.*, pp. 49–51.
6. Neil McElroy, *Vital Speeches of the Day*, April 1, 1961, pp. 370–373.
7. John C. Shearer, *High-Level Manpower in Overseas Subsidiaries* (Princeton, N.J.: Industrial Relations Section, Princeton University, 1960), p. 60.
8. John Fayerweather, *The Executive Overseas* (Syracuse, N.Y.: Syracuse University Press, 1959), pp. 158–159.
9. Lindeman and Armstrong, *op. cit.*, pp. 22–25.
10. Wolfgang G. Friedmann and George Kalmanoff (Eds.), *Joint International Business Ventures* (New York: Columbia University Press, 1961), pp. 20–22.
11. "Joint Venture Attitudes and Experience," *International Executive*, Summer, 1961, pp. 5–6.
12. Fayerweather, *op. cit.*, pp. 429–434.
13. Business International, *Investing & Licensing Conditions in 37 Countries* (New York: Haynes Publishing Company, 1960), p. 122.

Chapter 10

1. Fayerweather, *op. cit.*, pp. 133–160.

2. Richard D. Robinson, *Cases in International Business* (New York: Holt, Rinehart and Winston, Inc., 1962), pp. 78–99.
3. Benjamin A. Javits and Leon H. Keyserling, *The Peace by Investment Corporation* (Washington, D.C.: International Committee for Peace by Investment, 1961).
4. U.S. House of Representatives, Committee on Ways and Means, "A Plan for Waging the Economic War," *Private Foreign Investment* (Washington, D.C.: Government Printing Office, 1958), pp. 191–205.
5. Joseph P. Crockett, " 'Tax Sparing': A Legend Finally Reaches Print," *National Tax Journal*, June, 1958, pp. 148–149.

Chapter 11

1. Thomas Aitken, *A Foreign Policy for American Business* (New York: Harper & Brothers, 1961), p. 31.

■■■■■■■■■■■

Appendix

Basic Statistics of United States International Business

TABLE 1
United States Exports and Imports by Economic Classes
(In millions of dollars)

Year	Total	Crude materials	Crude food-stuffs	Manu-factured foodstuffs	Semi-manu-factures	Finished manu-factures
Exports						
1921–1925 Ave.	4,310	1,187	420	601	537	1,566
1926–1930 Ave.	4,688	1,114	300	456	663	2,126
1931–1935 Ave.	1,989	601	77	176	289	847
1936–1940 Ave.	3,167	603	119	175	611	1,658
1941–1945 Ave.	9,922	573	165	1,177	931	7,075
1946–1950 Ave.	11,673	1,630	973	1,198	1,295	6,576
1951	14,879	2,471	1,401	881	1,665	8,462
1952	15,049	1,982	1,369	736	1,619	9,341
1953	15,652	1,626	962	759	1,423	10,881
1954	14,981	1,899	741	832	1,819	9,691
1955	15,419	1,907	930	1,012	2,309	9,260
1956	18,940	2,515	1,332	1,264	2,775	11,054
1957	20,671	3,110	1,332	1,163	3,242	11,823
1958	17,745	2,139	1,280	1,102	2,277	10,947
1959	17,438	1,913	1,448	1,078	2,467	10,533
1960	20,300	2,586	1,639	1,117	3,522	11,435

TABLE 1 (*continued*)

Year	Total	Crude materials	Crude food-stuffs	Manu-factured foodstuffs	Semi-manu-factures	Finished manu-factures
Imports						
1921–1925 Ave.	3,450	1,290	383	448	609	720
1926–1930 Ave.	4,033	1,484	507	398	762	882
1931–1935 Ave.	1,704	493	266	234	319	393
1936–1940 Ave.	2,440	807	320	346	511	457
1941–1945 Ave.	3,476	1,147	569	400	735	624
1946–1950 Ave.	6,584	1,992	1,237	706	1,471	1,178
1951	10,817	3,365	2,077	1,022	2,459	1,896
1952	10,747	2,937	2,068	1,083	2,566	2,094
1953	10,779	2,613	2,185	1,108	2,678	2,194
1954	10,240	2,413	2,200	1,117	2,313	2,196
1955	11,337	2,845	1,998	1,118	2,777	2,599
1956	12,516	3,087	2,036	1,167	3,005	3,221
1957	12,951	3,211	2,020	1,272	2,920	3,527
1958	12,739	2,760	1,936	1,504	2,642	3,897
1959	14,994	3,097	1,824	1,599	3,306	5,168
1960	14,652	3,014	1,722	1,566	3,092	5,258

Source: Statistical Abstract of the United States.

TABLE 2
Value of Exports and Imports of Leading Commodities
by Areas for 1960
(In millions of dollars)

Commodity	Total	Canada	American republics	Western Europe	Far East	Other areas
Export totals[a]	$18,785	$3,699	$3,455	$6,279	$3,614	$1,738
Grains and preparations	1,650	55	175	540	566	314
Fats, oils, and oil seeds	748	63	61	389	178	58
Foodstuffs other than grains, fats, and oils	933	248	154	324	129	78
Cotton unmanufactured	988	46	15	479	419	30
Tobacco and manufactures	476	4	27	323	72	50
Machinery	4,088	1,054	1,010	977	638	409
Automobiles, parts and accessories	1,216	388	431	136	108	154
Chemicals and related products	1,661	277	399	562	317	106
Textile manufactures	695	156	132	177	117	113
Iron and steel-making raw materials	305	66	16	84	138	—
Iron and steel-mill products	611	133	142	184	99	53
Petroleum products	429	54	88	108	129	51
Coal and related products	362	129	23	155	54	—
Copper and copper-base alloys	378	6	23	270	79	2
Civilian aircraft	551	41	50	378	62	20
Other agricultural and nonagricultural exports	3,695	980	709	1,197	509	301
Import totals[a]	14,652	2,912	3,497	4,216	2,652	1,375
Coffee	1,003	—	874	—	3	126
Meat and edible animals	386	62	88	92	115	30
Cane sugar	507	—	370	1	125	11
Other foodstuffs	1,392	253	366	393	241	139
Crude rubber	322	—	1	—	271	50
Wool, unmanufactured	197	1	54	21	82	40
Nonferrous metals and ferroalloys	1,323	311	347	281	202	182
Paper and paper materials	1,099	977	1	106	11	4
Petroleum and products	1,543	107	827	1	60	548
Textile manufactures	932	10	38	369	492	23
Machinery, electrical and other	711	152	1	418	138	3
Automobiles, including parts	627	11	—	612	3	1
Sawmill products	310	273	15	—	18	3
Chemicals and related products	353	99	39	179	21	16
Iron and steel mill products	505	39	7	360	97	3
Other agricultural and nonagricultural imports	3,442	617	468	1,385	773	198

[a]The totals differ from those of Table 1 because of differences in methods of compiling the statistics.

Source: Statistical Abstract of the United States.

TABLE 3

United States Direct International Investments
by Major Industries as of December 31
(In millions of dollars)

Year	Manufacturing	Mining and smelting	Petroleum	Transportation, communication, and public utilities	Agriculture	Trade	Others	Total
1897	$ 100	$ 100	$ 100	$ 200	$ [a]	$ [a]	$ 100	$ 600
1914	500	700	300	400	400	[a]	400	2,700
1919	800	900	600	400	600	[a]	600	3,900
1929	1,813	1,185	1,117	1,610	880	388	555	7,528
1936	1,710	1,032	1,074	1,640	482	391	362	6,690
1945	2,671	1,064	1,538	1,357	518	671	550	8,369
1950	3,831	1,128	3,390	1,425	589	763	662	11,788
1955	6,349	2,209	5,849	1,614	[a]	1,282	2,010	19,313
1960	11,152	3,013	10,944	2,546	[a]	2,397	2,692	32,744

[a]Included in "Others."

Sources: E. R. Barlow & Ira T. Wender, *Foreign Investment & Taxation* (Englewood Cliffs, N. J.: Prentice-Hall, Inc., 1955), p. 11; and *Survey of Current Business.*

TABLE 4
United States Direct International Investments
by Major Industries by Regions as of December 31, 1960
(In millions of dollars)

Region	Manufacturing	Mining and smelting	Petroleum	Transportation, communication, and public utilities	Trade	Others	Total
Canada	$ 4,827	$1,329	$ 2,667	$ 645	$ 630	$1,100	$11,198
Latin-American Republics	1,610	1,155	2,882	1,131	718	870	8,365
Western Hemisphere dependencies	21	176	382	49	64	192	884
Europe	3,797	49	1,726	45	736	291	6,645
Africa	118	247	407	5	53	94	925
Asia	286	24	1,655	103	137	110	2,315
Oceania	494	33	372	1	58	36	994
International	—	—	851	567	—	—	1,418
Total	$11,152	$3,013	$10,944	$2,546	$2,397	$2,692	$32,744

Source: Survey of Current Business.

TABLE 5
Earnings of United States Direct Investments Abroad
(In millions of dollars)

Year	Dividends, interest, and branch profits	Undistributed profits retained abroad	Total earnings
1946	$ 589	$ 243	$ 832
1950	1,294	475	1,769
1955	1,912	898	2,811
1956	2,120	1,000	3,120
1957	2,313	1,017	3,330
1958	2,198	755	2,954
1959	2,206	1,089	3,295
1960	2,348	1,254	3,602

Source: Survey of Current Business.

TABLE 6
United States Balance of Payments
(In billions of dollars)

Year	Exports and imports	Net services	Private remittances	Government			Interest income	Private investment			Errors and omissions	Means of financing surplus or deficit	
				Net military expenses	Net loans	Grants		Net income	Net long-term investment	United States short-term capital		Gold	Dollars
1920	$ 3.1	$ —	$—0.6	$—0.1	$—0.2	$—0.1		$0.5		$—0.8	$—1.9	$ 0.1	$ —
1925	0.7	—0.4	—0.4	—	—	—		0.7		—0.7	—0.1	0.1	—0.1
1930	0.8	—0.5	—0.3	—	0.1	—		0.7		—0.5	0.3	—0.3	—0.3
1935	—0.1	—0.2	—0.2	—	—	—		0.4		0.9	0.4	—1.8	0.6
1940	1.5	—0.1	—0.2	—0.1	—0.1	—		0.4		0.1	1.3	—4.2	1.4
1945	7.3	1.8	—0.5	—2.3	—1.0	—6.6	$0.1	0.4	$—1.1	—0.6	—	0.5	2.2
1950	1.0	—	—0.4	—0.5	—0.2	—3.6	0.3	$1.2	—0.7	$—0.1	—	1.7	1.9
1954	2.4		—0.5	—2.4	0.1	—1.8	0.3	1.5	—0.7	—0.6	0.2	0.3	1.2
1955	2.8	—0.1	—0.4	—2.5	—0.3	—2.0		1.6		—0.2	0.4	—	1.1
1956	4.6	—	—0.5	—2.7	—0.6	—1.9	0.2	1.8	—2.0	—0.5	0.6	—0.3	1.3
1957	6.1	0.3	—0.5	—2.8	—0.9	—1.8	0.2	2.0	—2.5	—0.3	0.7	—0.8	0.3
1958	3.2	—0.1	—0.5	—3.1	—1.0	—1.8	0.3	1.9	—2.5	—0.3	0.4	2.3	1.2
1959	1.0	—0.2	—0.6	—2.8	—0.4	—1.8	0.3	1.9	—1.7	—0.1	0.5	0.7	3.2
1960	4.7	—0.3	—0.6	—2.7	—1.1	—1.9	0.3	2.0	—2.3	—1.3	—0.6	1.7	2.1

Source: Statistical Abstract of the United States.

Index

Afghanistan, economic aid, 115
AFL-CIO, 47
Africa, investments in, 178
Agricultural equipment, manufacture, 153–154
Agricultural products, United States exports, 166–167
Agriculture, overseas operations, 120, 129–131, 177
Aluminum, Russia, 114; tariffs, 32
American Cyanamid Co., 144
American International Association, 124
Argentina, investments in, 133, 148
Aswan Dam, 115, 118
Atul, 144
Australia, imports, 17; investments in, 6, 9, 128–129, 145, 151, 178
Automobiles, exports, 4, 8–10, 139, 176; overseas manufacture, 4, 8–10, 138, 139, 148–149; tariffs, 32

Balance of payments, investment earnings, 128–129, 180; Latin America, 129–133; United States, 1, 53, 65–100, 180
Ball-point pens, tariffs, 32
Bananas, imports, 36
Barlow, E. R., 5
Base companies, 50–64
Belgium, taxes, 63
Benoit, Emile, 17, 28, 29
Benzene, imports, 112
Bicycles, imports, 33, 46
Boggs, Hale, 61
Bowater Paper Co., 77
Brazil, investments in, 10, 128, 140, 141, 143, 147, 148, 153, 154
Britain, currency, 96, 98; exchange rate, 68, 84; fish embargo, 116; trade, 46, 110, 113
Brookings Institution, 32, 34
Burma, exports, 117
Business Council for International Understanding, 135

Business Week, 11, 78
"Buy American" regulations, 33

Canada, economy, 165; investments in, 136–141, 143, 151, 153, 178; tariffs, 41; trade, 15, 139, 176
Capitalism, attitudes toward, 133–134
Cárdenas, Lazaro, 121–123
Casablanca Bloc, 27
Castro, Fidel, 160
Caterpillar Tractor Co., 1, 5
Celanese Corp., 148
Cement, prices, 17
Central America, common market, 27; investments in, 125, 134
Ceylon, trade, 117
Chamber of Commerce, Mexico, 126; United States, 23
Chambers of Commerce, American, 135
Chemicals, equipment, 106–107, 109–110; exports, 4, 176; overseas manufacture, 138; tariffs, 32
Chile, exports, 118; investments in, 139, 152, 153
China (communist), trade, 102, 117, 139
Chinaware, imports, 33; labor costs, 39
Chrysler Corp., 8
Coal, exports, 68, 176
Cocoa, Russian imports, 116
Colombia, investments in, 144
Commerce, United States Department of, 26, 72, 129
Committee for Economic Development, 155
Common markets, 27–29
Comparative advantage, 36
Control, management, 82–83, 142–145, 148
Controls, export, 107–111; foreign exchange, 88
Coordinating Committee (COCOM), 108

Copper, investments, 139–140, 152; trade, 118
Cotton, exports, 68; Russian trade, 115, 117
Cotton textiles, imports, 33; tariffs, 32
Creole Petroleum Corp., 124–125
Cuba, investments in, 160

David, Donald K., 155
Denmark, taxes, 63
"Depressed Areas" Bill, 48
Development Loan Fund, 74
Díaz, Porfirio, 120–121
Diefenbaker, John G., 143
Dillon, Douglas, 54, 59, 62, 80, 81
Dividends, payments to United States, 79, 179, 180
Dollar, as an international currency, 96
Dollars, foreign holdings of, 85, 94, 180
Dortmund-Horder, 19
duPont (E. I.) de Nemours & Co., 106–107, 147

Ealing Corp., 113
Economic aid, Russian, 115; United States, 73–77, 115
Egypt, Russian aid, 115, 117; trade, 103
Eisenhower, Dwight D., 61, 106
Electrical equipment, overseas manufacture, 138; imports, 33–34, 176
Employment, United States, 1, 20, 34, 39–40
"Escape Clause," 45
Europe, economy, 78, 82, 165; investments in, 10, 81, 151, 153, 159, 178; trade, 29, 68, 111, 176
European Economic Community (EEC), 27–29, 44, 78
European Free Trade Association (EFTA), 27
Exchange rates, 38, 68–69, 84
Export-Import Bank, 24, 74
Exports, credit insurance, 24; Latin America, 129–133; licensing, 107–108; by overseas operations, 141; United States, 1–30, 39, 57–60, 67–70, 79, 82–83, 165–167, 174, 176
Expropriation, 121–123, 159–161
Extractive industries, overseas operations, 120–136, 139, 152

Fiat, 9–10
Film rentals, 73
Finance, management policy, 145
Financing, investments, 154, 156
Firestone Tire & Rubber Co., 162
Fish, trade, 116
Ford Motor Co., 8, 139, 140, 148–149
Foreign Business Corporation, 61
Foreign Commerce Weekly, 26
Foreign Credit Insurance Association (FCIA), 24
France, currency reserves, 93; exchange rate, 68; investments in, 159; prices, 17; taxes, 63
Fur, imports, 113

Gehrels, Franz, 39
General Agreement on Tariffs and Trade (GATT), 44
General Electric Co., 20, 155
General Motors Corp,. 4, 8–10, 55, 128–129, 140, 148–149
Germany, currency, 96; economy, 64; exchange rate, 69, 84; investment in, 161; military expenditures, 76; prices, 17; taxes, 57–60, 63; trade, 12, 21–22, 24–25, 111, 116, 118
Glassware, labor costs, 39
Gloversville, 35, 36
Gloves, imports, 33, 35
Gold, price, 68–69; Russia, 112; transfers, 83, 180; United States reserves, 91, 92, 94
Gomulka, Wladyslaw, 102
Goodrich (B. F.) Co., 144
Gordon Commission, 41, 137, 143
Gore, Albert, 1, 80
Guinea, investments in, 152

Hatter's fur, imports, 33
Heinz, H. J., II, 6
Hermes, 24
Hong Kong, costs, 40
House of Representatives, Ways and Means Committee, 54
Hull, Cordell, 31
Humphrey, George, 157
Huson, Gordon, 140

Ibáñez del Campo, Carlos, 118
Iceland, trade, 116
Imports, controls, 70; injured industries, 34–36, 43–49; United

Imports, *(cont.)*
    States, 31–49, 67–70, 112–113, 116,
      165–167, 175, 176
India, imports, 17, 116; investments
    in, 6, 9, 138, 144–147, 153, 161–163
Indonesia, exports, 118; taxes, 134
Industria Electrica de Mexico, 144
Inland Steel Co., 19
Interest rates, 84, 87
International Executive, The, 80, 144
International Harvester Co., 51, 153
International Monetary Fund, 91, 97
International Telephone and Telegraph
    Co., 73
Investments, direct, 1–11, 50–64,
    77–83, 93, 120–167, 177, 178;
    earnings from, 81–82, 127–133, 145,
    179, 180; guarantees, 159–161;
    by local capital, 143; portfolio,
    77, 79, 93; short-term capital,
    83–89, 93, 180
Iraq, 118
Italy, trade, 111, 113

Japan, economy, 165; investments in,
    126, 147, 153; trade, 12, 22, 37, 46
Javits, Jacob, 155
Johnson, Harry, 137
Johnson Act of 1934, 112
Johnson & Johnson, 147
Joint ventures, 80, 82, 143–148

Kaiser Industries, 133, 143, 147
Kennedy, John F., 49, 53
Khrushchev, Nikita, 101, 104, 112
Korolev, Dmitri, 104–105
Kravis, Irving, 40
Kreinin, Mordechai, 34
Krupp, 111

Labor, costs, 38–39; foreign, 134;
    Mexico, 121–124; United States, 49
Latin America, economy, 165;
    investments in, 9, 129–133, 160–161,
    163, 178; trade, 129–133, 176
Latin American Free Trade
    Association (LAFTA), 27
Lend-Lease program, 101, 106
Licensing, 80, 82
Loans, Russian, 115; United States
    government, 74, 92, 93, 180

Machine tools, exports, 21
Machinery, exports, 4, 79, 103, 176;
    investments, 138

Managerial personnel, 123–124, 141
Manufacturing, overseas, 1–11, 80,
    125–135, 137–164, 166–167, 177, 178
Manufacturing Chemists' Association,
    109
Marketing, management policies,
    145–146
Marshall Plan, 20, 159
McCoy, Horace B., 48
McDonald, David, 47
McElroy, Neil, 141
Merchant Marine, 70
Merck and Co., 147
Mexico, economy, 165; imports, 15;
    investments in, 10, 120–124, 126,
    128, 138, 141–143, 147–149, 154;
    petroleum industry, 120–124
Middle East, investments in, 152;
    petroleum, 116, 118
Military expenditures, 73–77, 180
Miller, Raymond, 134
Mining, Mexico, 123; overseas,
    129–131, 137–138, 152, 177, 178
Minneapolis-Moline, 154, 156
Monrovia group, 27
Musical instruments, imports, 33

National Cash Register Co., 141
National Industrial Conference Board,
    53
National Planning Association, 35,
    124, 135, 136, 140, 143
Nationalism, 133
Nehru, Jawaharlal, 162

Olin Mathieson Corp., 152
Olivetti, 8, 77
Organization for Economic Coopera-
    tion and Development (OECD), 77

Pakistan, taxes, 156–158
Parke-Davis and Co., 147
Patents, Russia, 106
Peace by Investment Corporation, 155
"Peril Point" clause, 45, 47
Petroleum, Mexico, 120–124; overseas
    operations, 121–125, 129–131, 134,
    137–138, 152, 160, 177, 178; Russia,
    114; trade, 33, 68, 114, 116, 117
Pharmaceuticals, investments, 6, 138
Philco Corp., 2
Piquet, Howard S., 34
Poland, trade, 102

Positive List, 107–108
Postal services, 73
Potato chips, 105
Prices, export, 17, 69, 75; foreign controls, 134; United States, 87, 89
Productivity, 19–20, 40
Profits, from direct investments, 156–161, 179, 180; reinvestment, 50–64, 179
Public Law 480 (PL 480), 74
Public relations, 135

Randall Commission, 47
Remington Rand, 7
Remissions, private, 73, 180
Robinson, Richard, 139
Roosevelt, Franklin D., 104
Rueff, Jacques, 96
Russia, economic aid, 115; economy, 103–105; trade, 101–119

Quotas, import, 33, 70

Salant, Walter, 34
Saudi Arabia, investments in, 152
Scott, J. B., 110, 112
Sears, Roebuck and Co., 126–127, 145
Sewing machines, 126
Shipping, expenditures, 70–71
Singer Manufacturing Co., 126, 159
Smith-Corona-Marchant, Inc., 7
Smoot-Hawley Tariff Act of 1930, 31, 42, 113
Socialism, 134, 162
Southeast Asian States, 27
Sovereignty, 55–56
Squibb (Division of Olin Mathieson Chemical Corp.), 155
Stalin, Joseph, 103
State, United States Department of, 25, 135
Steel, exports, 68, 176; prices, 17, 20; tariffs, 32
Stockholm Convention, 27
Strackbein, Oscar R., 34
Suez crisis, 68
Switzerland, currency, 96; laws, 56–57, taxes, 52, 53, 58–59
Syria, 118

Tariff Commission, 45–46, 116
Tariffs, Canada, 141; copper, 118; Europe, 28–29; fish, 116; United States, 29, 50–64, 70, 72, 141

Tax havens, 50–64, 157
Tax sparing, 157–158
Taxes, foreign, 134, 156–158; treaties, 158; United States, 50–64, 156–158
Technical aid, United States, 75
Texaco, Inc., 160, 163
Textiles, imports, 35, 46
Tin, Russia, 114
Tires, exports, 140; overseas manufacture, 138, 162; Russia, 111
Tourists, 71–72
Tractors, manufacture, 153–154
Trade Agreements Act, 31, 42–43, 113
Trade Relations Council, 48
Transportation, expenditures, 70–71
Treasury, United States Department of, 50, 53, 54, 61, 157
Treaty of Rome, 27
Triffin, Robert, 98
Trousers, imports, 35
Turkey, investments in, 154–155
Typewriters, manufacture, 7

Underwood Act of 1913, 42
Underwood Corp., 8
Union Carbide Corp., 143
United Fruit Co., 122, 125, 134
United States government, economic aid, 155; expenditures, 73–77, 180; export expansion program, 23; investment guarantees, 159–161; private investment support, 121, 135, 154

Venezuela, exports, 118; petroleum operations, 124–125
Vickers-Armstrong, 110
Volkswagen, 9

Wages, 18–19, 37; United States, 40, 70
Walton's, 145
Washing machines, 64
Watches, labor costs, 39; tariffs, 32
Wender, Ira T., 5
Westinghouse Electric Corp., 144
Wool, imports, 33; labor costs, 39
World Bank (International Bank for Reconstruction and Development), 93

Young, J. H., 41

Zinc, imports, 33